I am so thankful Janet opened her life and told her story so others can find love, truth, and freedom. It is time for the church to be rightly related to all of its children. *Called Out* is part of this happening.

—LISA BEVERE, AUTHOR AND SPEAKER
KISSED THE GIRLS, FIGHT LIKE A GIRL, MESSENGER
INTERNATIONAL

In this world, sexuality is exposed and exploited in a mixing bowl of confusion and uncertainty. Where the homosexual community would have you believe that they are victims of their sexual preference based on design rather than choice, a clear voice comes to us from one who has lived their lifestyle and has overcome the turmoil through the love of Jesus Christ. This is a must read, not only for those who have been exposed to the gay lifestyle or others who question their sexuality, but also to those who are called to minister in the twenty-first century.

—PASTOR MARVIN L. WINANS
SENIOR PASTOR
PERFECTING CHURCH, DETROIT, MI

Janet Boynes has an all-too-common story to tell about how a dysfunctional and abusive family produces a needy adult. Her story will not shock you; it will just help you see the reasons why many people turn to drugs and homosexuality.

But this isn't just an autobiography. Janet uses her experience to speak to the heart of the matter. She gives clear concise advice to those who either are gay or know gay individuals—which includes most of us. *Called Out* provides a sounding board for the questions most of us ask. There are no gray areas with Janet. She helps us point the accusing finger back at ourselves to see what we are doing to arrest the problems of our society.

The profound message Janet shares is a simple one: if the church solves its own problems, instead of wasting time sending mixed signals about the gay lifestyle; if the church learns to love as Jesus loved; if the church becomes healthy enough; then it can truly minister grace to those who are sick and fulfill God's purpose.

You should take the time not only to read this book but to give it to those who do not understand the mind of the homosexual. Great job, Janet!

—BISHOP HARRY R. JACKSON, JR.
SENIOR PASTOR, HOPE CHRISTIAN CHURCH
PRESIDENT, HIGH IMPACT LEADERSHIP COALITION

Janet Boynes is an amazing and inspirational example of the power of faith to transform and heal. Her life is evidence of God's unceasing love for all His children, and her ministry offers hope to those seeking a way out of homosexuality. Her teaching is bold and compassionate; she speaks the truth of God's grace and mercy, and she speaks from experience. Our society needs to hear her story.

—GARY L. BAUER
CHRISTIAN CONSERVATIVE ACTIVIST

Janet Boynes's life is an amazing testimony to God's grace and truth. *Called Out* proclaims that freedom from homosexuality is not only possible, but inevitable for anyone who chooses to surrender their sexuality to the lordship of Jesus Christ. Janet is a good friend and a hero of the faith.

—ALAN CHAMBERS
PRESIDENT, EXODUS INTERNATIONAL

Janet Boynes's autobiographical book, *Called Out*, is an inspiring story of God's grace, as well as of the real possibility of change for those trapped by homosexual desires. With blunt honesty, Janet tells the often heart-wrenching story of the hardship and abuse she suffered early in life, which led her to descend into lesbian relationships. But she also shares how God used the persistent love of believers to call her to faith in Christ and call her out of her sin. Her moving personal story is then followed by sound and compassionate advice to those dealing with homosexuality in their own lives, the lives of family members, and in the church. I recommend *Called Out* to anyone interested in knowing how God's love can transform the lives of those wrestling with the tragedy of homosexuality.

—Tony Perkins
President, Family Research Council

Janet's story provides compelling evidence that it is possible to overcome any life-controlling issue, including sexual abuse and homosexuality. When Janet visited Mercy Ministries and shared her testimony with our staff and girls, the freedom of her new life was evident. Janet is a great communicator and a wonderful example of the life-transforming power of Jesus Christ. It is my prayer that as you read this book, you will be moved with compassion for those who are still struggling.

—Nancy Alcorn
President and Founder
Mercy Ministries

Called
Out

Called Out

JANET BOYNES

CREATION HOUSE
A STRANG COMPANY

CALLED OUT by Janet Boynes
Published by Creation House
A Strang Company
600 Rinehart Road
Lake Mary, Florida 32746
www.creationhouse.com

Unless otherwise marked, Scripture quotations are from the Holy Bible, New International Version. Copyright © 1973, 1978, 1984, International Bible Society. Used by permission.

Scripture quotations marked NKJV are from the New King James Version of the Bible. Copyright © 1979, 1980, 1982 by Thomas Nelson, Inc., publishers. Used by permission.

Author photo by Jolene Bertrand, www.avalonphotoinfo.com

Author's note: Names and circumstance have been changed to protect identities.

Design Director: Bill Johnson
Cover design by Amanda Potter

Library of Congress Control Number: 2008926036
International Standard Book Number: 978-1-59979-385-6

First Edition

08 09 10 11 12 — 9 8 7 6 5 4 3 2 1
Printed in the United States of America

To our Father God, Lord of love,
To our dearest Jesus, love's sweet sacrifice,
To our precious Spirit, the cry of our beating hearts,
Let these words we have written, whether all or in part,
Penetrate to the soul, to the eternity of the lives,
Touching all for Your glory enthroned above.

For my brother, Robert.

Acknowledgments

To my dearest mother, who has loved me throughout all my trials and tribulations from adolescence to adulthood. Despite your disagreement to my prior lifestyle, your steadfast devotion to me is unquestionable, unparalleled, and beyond measure.

To Pastor Greg and Maple Grove Assembly of God families, thank you for your unfailing love and support in my walk with God.

George and Barb, your love and support have never wavered. Thank you for believing in me and the ministry God has called me to.

To the Carmichael family, whose constant love, support, and friendship to my life and purpose have never dwindled in my lowest lows or tapered in my highest of highs.

Marcus and Michele, when we met, our friendship was instant, and you never left my side when things got tough. To watch your walk with God gives me strength, courage, and hope.

Ben, you believed in me when I didn't believe in myself. Thank you for everything.

Too many friends and family to mention, thank you all for your loyalty and love that carried me through some tough times in my transformation.

Jesus, thank you for giving me a second chance and calling me out of darkness into your marvelous light.

CONTENTS

PART I
THE STORY

Chapter 1

GROWING UP

JANET, I DON'T WANT YOU GROWIN' UP TO BE NO LESBIAN. I don't want you to end up like any of them other neighborhood girls."

Even today, those words echo in my ears. My mother was strict, tough, and didn't think twice about telling anyone exactly what she thought. She loved us kids, but often didn't know how to show it. She had a hard childhood and much of her toughness was inherited from her own mother. When she yelled at us, her words usually did more harm than good.

I didn't have much of a relationship with my mother. There were seven children in our family and we never really had a consistent father figure. My biological father was a married man who had had an affair with my mother and my siblings all shared three different fathers. My mother worked hard to help support us, but it also seemed to me as if she picked her favorite children. I wasn't one of the favorites and I often wondered if she even liked me.

Life isn't always easy. I began learning that lesson early in my childhood. I was born April 5, 1958 in Norristown, Pennsylvania. Our family was poor and we lived on welfare most of our lives. We received food stamps once a month so we could go shopping at the grocery store, but the food we were able to get with the stamps was simple. I remember

1

my mother coming home with big blocks of cheese, bags of cornmeal and rice, and peanut butter in a can.

We lived in the middle of the city in a row home. Our house was connected to the neighbors' houses and we could hear every sound they made. If one house became infected with rodents or roaches, we were almost sure to get them as well. I had to chase mice and cockroaches with a broom more than once. The row home was small and I had to share a room with my sisters Patricia and Mildred. My brothers Robert, Henry, and Mitchell also shared a room while my older brother Jesse had a room to himself.

When it was time to play with kids in the neighborhood, we had to be sure to stay close to the house so my mother could see us. She had to have absolute control over our lives and we could never play kickball in the alley or play hide-and-seek because she always had to have an eye on us. She constantly threatened us to make us afraid of disobeying her.

My mother was a strict disciplinarian and a perfectionist, always demanding the house be kept spotless. She told us to clean everything right the first time so that we wouldn't have to go back and do it again. I quickly learned not to take short-cuts and to do everything the right way from the beginning. My mother sometimes literally inspected our work with a white glove and if the cleaning did not meet her approval, she beat us and made us clean it again until we did it right.

My siblings and I knew better than to try doing things behind our mother's back. All of us children lived in fear of her. If we did something wrong, she always found out. We believed her when she told us that she had eyes in the back of her head. Even if she didn't do something to us right away, she had a long memory, and we always "got whipped." Weeks or months sometimes went by before we were punished because she wanted to wait until we didn't remember and weren't looking before she got us. I remember getting slapped in the face more than once for something I had done weeks before. Our beatings were spankings with belts, extension cords, or broom handles on our naked butts.

Even though my mother didn't respect our physical boundaries, her words were sometimes even more hurtful than her beatings. She called us whores and bitches to try to make us behave. Both my mother and my grandmother told me I looked like a tomboy and that I should try acting more like a girl. I was a stocky little girl and their words began finding a place in my heart, despite my best efforts to shut them out. After constantly hearing the same negative message about myself from so many different sources, I began to believe it. Eventually those words began to control my life.

I became convinced that I was a bad kid and deserved all of the beating and name-calling I received. I grew up hating my mother and used to lay awake at night, thinking of ways to kill her before running away. I never tried any of my plans because I was literally afraid that my mother would come back from the dead to get me.

Shortly after I was born, my mother began dating a carpenter named Gus. Though she never married Gus, they had three children together and he lived with us for a long time.

Because I felt rejected by my mother, I reached out to Gus. I became Daddy's girl. He had pet names for me, calling me "Fats" and "Gonnit," which was his affectionate way of saying Janet. I remember him coming home and calling out, "Where's my Gonnit?"

Things didn't go very well between Gus and my mother. She wasn't an easy woman to live with and she absolutely dominated Gus with her strong personality. She often embarrassed him in front of other people to make herself look better and constantly looked for ways to start arguments. Many of their fights turned physical when she grabbed perfume bottles, dishes, and anything else that was nearby to throw at Gus. He began drinking and staying out of the house until the early morning just to avoid her, but she waited up for him and then fought with him when he came back home.

I remember staying awake at night listening to their arguments echo along the wood-paneled halls of our house. My siblings and I were able to handle the arguments, but when we heard things begin to hit the walls, we knew we were in for a long, sleepless night. Even though I loved Gus, when I grew older I got involved in their fights and tried to protect my mother by threatening and hitting him.

My home life turned me into a tough little girl. I did not want anyone to hurt me ever again and so I decided I had to hurt others before they could cause me any pain. I became abusive when I started school, slapping my kindergarten teacher in the face and bullying the other children. When I was in sixth grade, I joined the Safety Patrol and became one of the leaders, though my time in leadership did not last long after I became angry with a student and kicked him in his private parts.

I did not make many friends in school and quickly received the titles of "bully" and "tomboy," names that made me proud. Other girls didn't want to be called tomboy because they wanted to date boys, but I didn't care because I wanted to *fight* boys. And that's exactly what I did. Everyone was afraid of me because I beat the boys up and the girls wouldn't have anything to do with me.

My fighting wasn't limited to school; I also fought with my brothers and sisters at home. I liked to fight so much that Gus bought two sets of boxing gloves for us one Christmas. Whenever I got into an argument with one of my siblings, we went down into the basement, put on the gloves, and fought until one of us had knocked the other unconscious.

I hated everything that had to do with being a little girl. I would not cook because I was convinced that cooking was for girls so I traded my cooking chores with my sisters for their cleaning chores. I never wanted to play with dolls when I got them. Instead, I played with my brothers' cars, trucks, baseball cards, and any other toys that they left lying around the house. If there was a football game being played, I was right in the middle of it and I always wanted to play tackle. I constantly carried a basketball around, just like I saw many of the boys in school doing. I refused to wear a bra because the guys didn't have to and I didn't think it was fair that I should be forced to wear one. I also wouldn't wear girls' shoes, but wore sneakers instead. I longed to be with and be like boys and men because I thought that they were stronger than women and didn't experience pain and suffering.

When I was about twelve-years-old, I discovered that I had a different father than my brothers and sisters. I had known that Robert and Patricia had a different father, but Gus had always been the man I called Daddy and so it never occurred to me that I might be different from my siblings. Robert and I were at a parade one day when a man walked out of the crowd and started talking to me.

"Hi Janet," he said to me.

I turned to Robert and asked, "Who is *this* guy?"

Robert knew the truth, but he just shrugged. "Ask him," he said.

When I asked the man, he said, "I'm John. I'm your father."

He then began asking me if I knew certain girls at school. When I recognized the names, he told me that they were my sisters.

I didn't believe him so I ran back home to ask my mother, who took me to see Gus at work. They told me then that I did have a different dad than all of my brothers and sisters. I was crushed. I felt betrayed. Suddenly, my place in the family had shifted and I didn't know who I was anymore.

I started noticing the slight differences in the way my siblings and I looked. I thought that I looked more like my father's daughters than I looked like the rest of my siblings. I didn't even know if my mother was really my biological mother.

My mother hadn't wanted me to have much contact with my father because she was afraid he would move me away and I would never come back. I tried to see him on my own from time to time after I grew a little older, but we never established a close relationship. My discomfort at home grew and I began seeking love and reassurance from outside my family.

I was interested in boys, as most little girls are, but my masculine features and the fact that I beat them up kept most of the boys away from me. I had crushes on boys, but I never told anyone. I was too afraid of rejection to take any action myself. None of the boys wanted to be with me in the open, but many of them wanted to have sex with me behind closed doors. Since the nice boys were too afraid to approach me, I set my sights on boys at least two years younger than me and we snuck into the alleyway to make out and smoke. I was looking for love and for something that would make me feel good and I knew that they would give me attention because I was an older girl.

Several months after I found out about my real father, I drew the attention of someone older, but he was *much* older. Bobby was the father of my sister Patricia and my brother Robert and we often went to visit him. One day he sent my two sisters to the store, but made me stay behind with him. That day changed my life. While we were alone in his house, he started touching me in areas that no man should ever touch a little child.

I hated myself for being so weak that I couldn't even protect myself from him. He drove around my block later that day and I was sure he was looking for me to make sure I didn't tell anyone what he did to me. I didn't tell my mother what had happened because I was too afraid of what she would do to me if she found out. I was afraid that she wouldn't believe me and that she would beat or kill me instead.

Only a few months later, I was raped by an altar boy at church. I went to the basement to go to the bathroom after the service and he followed me, yanking me into the boiling room. He pulled my pants down and attacked me. When I got home, I was so afraid that I might be pregnant that I actually told my mother about the incident because she had always threatened that she would put us in a girls' home if we got pregnant. I didn't want her to think it was my fault if I became pregnant. I took a pregnancy test, which turned out negative, and my mother called the priest, who came to our house with the boy and his grandmother. I didn't say a word the entire time, but they made the boy apologize to me.

My thirteenth birthday passed and I continued getting into trouble. My friend Sharonda smoked a lot of pot and her mother let her smoke it at home, so I began smoking pot with her. I had learned about drugs by visiting my brother Jesse's room as I was growing up. I smelled pot when he came in at night and so I began going into his room to find his drugs. He kept cigarettes and pot stashed under his bed or in his closet. When I reached my teen years, I started stealing from him and using the drugs myself.

The pot smoking quickly led to the use of other drugs and soon I was smoking cigarettes, taking speed in the form of diet pills, and using acid, cocaine, and PCP. My friends and I mixed marijuana with the PCP so that we could have hallucinations. I never refused the drugs because everybody was doing them and I wanted to finally fit in somewhere. I smoked pot in my home after my mother went to work and before I went to school.

My drug use led me to start stealing money from Gus after he came home drunk. He had a two-pocket apron filled with nails for carpentry and he also kept his money in it, so I raided it whenever I was able. Because I stole from him after he came home, when he woke up the next morning, he never noticed that his money was missing because he thought he had spent it at the bar the night before.

Before I turned fourteen, my family was visited with another hardship. While most of my family was at a pancake jamboree, our house caught on fire because my youngest sister, who had stayed home, threw a match in the closet. The resulting blaze left us with nothing to salvage.

My family was forced to move in with my Grandma Willis for a year while Gus worked on rebuilding our home. The only good thing that I remember happening because of our move was that my mother and Gus didn't fight because they were not living together while the house was being rebuilt.

Despite everything that had been happening throughout my childhood, I remember always thinking that there had to be something better in life than what I had experienced. I just didn't know what that something better was. I had only limited exposure to God as a child. There was a bus that came down our street every week with an announcement for a movie about Jesus blaring over its loudspeaker. It was held at a local community center and it was one of the few things that my mother ever let us go to alone. My mother was an Episcopalian and forced all of us kids to go to church every Sunday. We even took catechism classes but, although I learned about the Bible, I never understood the concept of salvation. I didn't feel as if I knew God and I was absolutely sure that I didn't like church.

There was a church near my grandmother's house and I remember always hearing singing and seeing people dressed in white going into the church. I often poked my head through the doors of the church to see what was so special about it. Several girls I knew from school saw me one day and began talking to me about God, but I wasn't ready for that kind of life. I had difficulty understanding why they went to church every Wednesday, Saturday, and Sunday. However, I knew they had something different in their lives than I did and I often thought about what they said.

I was constantly looking for ways to escape from the events in my life. Drugs and smoking couldn't fill the void so I became heavily involved in sports at my school. I joined the basketball team during the winter and the track team during the spring. I was a fast runner and I did well in sports, making the headlines in our local newspapers. No matter how much I excelled, my mother came to only one game in my entire high school career. I understand today that she couldn't come because she worked at a hospital during the evenings and had no transportation, but it still hurt me as a young girl. It would have meant so much to me for her to have seen me succeed at something.

School was a far different world than sports. I hated studying and I did just enough to get by, sometimes even cheating so I could play in basketball games and practice with my team. I was such a good athlete that my teachers pushed me through school and I actually became an All-American basketball player, even though I never did my schoolwork. I still got into trouble often and spent a lot of time in the principal's office. I was suspended three to four times a month during junior high.

Getting into trouble didn't concern me because my Aunt Barbara came and helped me get back into school after being suspended. She knew my mother would be hard on me and so she tried to help me out whenever she was able. Eventually, however, the principal told me that I couldn't call on my aunt anymore; he wanted to talk to my mother. *That* terrified me. More than once, my mother came to get me at school and slapped me in front of the principal, yelling at me for getting in trouble again.

In eighth grade, my troublemaking turned into a blessing. After I had acted up in English class, my teacher, Cindy, made me stay after school. Cindy was one of those few people who really cared about those around her and she took me under her wing. She told me that I had a lot of potential; it was the first time in my life that anyone had spoken anything positive about me. I started to hang out with her after school. From that point forward, whenever I got into trouble at school, I was always sent to Cindy because no one else could deal with me. All the other teachers wanted me kicked out of school, but Cindy was the only one who saw beyond my rough exterior to my heart.

Weeks and months went by and I spent my days after school playing sports and my weekends with Cindy. My mother almost never said no to my spending time with her because she saw her as a positive influence on my life. I went bowling with Cindy and her husband and they often attended my basketball games. They also taught me how to play card games like pinochle, poker, and bidwist. We spent many late nights in their kitchen playing pinochle and I was proud whenever I was able to beat Cindy because she was so competitive.

Even though I felt Cindy had made me a part of her family, I still tested her love to see if it was real. I tried to go to her house while I was high, but she wouldn't stand for it. She put me in the car and drove me straight back home. Her tough but fair love became a singular ray of light in my otherwise dark world. She always called me by my last name and would tell me, "You have a future, Boynes. You have real potential."

My only happy times in those days were with Cindy. My home life was still a mess. We all lived in constant fear of my mother and we each found different ways to cope with that fear. Gus continued to drink and Patricia started to do so as well. Jesse was always high on pot and hash and Robert began staying out until the early morning.

Toward the end of my eighth grade year, I began noticing something strange. One by one, I was gradually losing pairs of my shoes and certain articles of my clothing began disappearing as well. I asked everyone in my family if they knew what had happened to them. No one knew, but Patricia mentioned that she was also missing clothes. Finally, a knock on the door one day solved the mystery.

My mother answered the door and the person at the door told her that my brother Robert was secretly spending his evenings as a cross-dresser named Barbara. My mother became angry and wouldn't believe it until someone took her to see Robert one night. He was dressed up in women's clothes and wearing my shoes. He cross-dressed at night for various men with whom he was involved.

Robert was smart, but he had always been passive, sensitive, and feminine. When he was younger, he had played football and run track, but later he was more interested in singing and talent shows. He constantly craved attention and would say things like, "Mom, you don't like me." With such a large family, she wasn't able to give any of us much attention and we lacked positive male role models who might have been able to counteract her domineering personality.

When Robert announced that he was gay, my mother kicked him out of the house for a while and he went to live with my Aunt Barbara. There was no convincing him to change because he had made up his mind and he had already been involved sexually with several men. Even though my mother wasn't very happy about his decision, the rest of us weren't bothered very much, except for when he stole our clothes.

Robert's announcement was far from my first exposure to homosexuality. I didn't have many friends, but many of the friends I did have were lesbians. Sharonda lived across the street and helped me get cigarettes and pot, but my mother didn't approve of me hanging out with her because she was a lesbian.

Still, I became more curious as time went on, but I never dared to explore a lesbian lifestyle for fear of my mother. I still dated, but my relationships were short-lived and often messy. My longest relationship was with a boy named Steven. He took me to prom, but we broke up soon afterward because I found out that he had been cheating on me with another girl. When I found out about the other girl, I vandalized Steven's car and flattened all his tires.

I started going to house parties, continuing my bad habits. I tried alcohol a few times, but I never liked it as much as smoking and drugs. I had to be careful at the parties, though, because my mother had a strict ten o'clock curfew. I only broke it a few times and I regretted it every time because my mother came looking for me. After basketball practice one evening, I went to a restaurant with my friends. It was later than usual and as I sat on a stool, smoking and talking with my friends, my mother came up behind me. When she saw me smoking, she walked up and slapped me in the face so hard it knocked me off my stool to the ground.

My mother still fought with Gus as well. He continued his drinking habits, and while I was still in high school he was involved in a car accident one night, killing someone in the process. He was forced to serve time in a state hospital and receive alcohol treatment. It was suggested that he and my mother also get relationship counseling, but she refused. When Gus saw that my mother wasn't about to change, he decided that he couldn't go back into that environment and still stay sober. He eventually found someone half his age and married her after he was released from the hospital.

For all of her beatings, cussing, and the fear that she inspired, I know that, deep down, my mother loved us children. Even though she had a rough exterior and didn't know how to express her love, she was softhearted on the inside. She didn't make much money, but she always tried to make sure that we had a good Christmas with presents every year.

She surprised me one day when she said suddenly, "I'm tough on you, Janet, because I want you to graduate. I don't want you to have the life that I had growing up."

I did graduate. Despite the toughness of my mother and because of the steady influence of Cindy, I graduated on a spring day in 1976. Cindy and her husband moved to Minnesota for an administrative job, but as it turned out, she would still have a role to play in my life. My mother was right as well. I ended up having a much different life than she did, though at that point I don't think either one of us expected what was still to come.

Chapter 2
ALMOST MARRIED

After high school, I enrolled at Cheney State College in Pennsylvania. Before I left, my mother used her savings and limited investments to give me as much money as she was able to help me pay for college. It wasn't much, but it was all she had and I will be forever grateful for what she did.

I wanted to play basketball at Cheney, so I tried out for the team and made the roster. I played well, but I had a hard time keeping my grades up because I used too many drugs and stayed out late partying too often. I was still smoking pot and I used it all the more when I arrived at college. I wasn't happy with life and my unresolved childhood kept me from looking for love in the right places.

During a basketball tournament in Savannah, Georgia, I met a man named Donald. We began talking, exchanged phone numbers, and began a relationship. Donald bought me a plane ticket and flew me to Georgia to see him every weekend I didn't have a practice or a game. I eventually found out that he was able to pay for my airline tickets because he was a drug dealer. I didn't care, however, because Donald was good to me and provided me with all the attention and drugs that I wanted.

Despite Donald's attention, my life still wasn't where I wanted it to be. I knew that I was missing something vital.

When my drug use made me ineligible to play basketball during my third year at Cheney, I knew that something had to change.

I called Cindy in Minnesota and told her that I was unable to play basketball, that my grades were getting worse, and that I needed to move. After hearing my situation, she offered to buy me a one-way plane ticket to Minneapolis so I could begin to turn my life around. Realizing how badly I needed the change, I broke up with Donald, took Cindy's offer, and moved to Minneapolis.

Cindy let me stay with her for about a month and helped me apply to Concordia Bible College, which I would attend for the next year. I began taking classes and even enrolled in a New Testament Bible course. I also played as a walk-on for the Concordia basketball team, finally able to return to the sport I loved.

Even though I was attending a Christian school, I couldn't escape my past. Temptations and desires began creeping up on me and a girl named Leanna began to catch my eye. I still associated with guys and was attracted to them, but I could feel myself changing. Lesbianism was always something in the back of my mind, just waiting for me to embrace it.

Even though we were just friends, I became convinced that I was in love with Leanna and began writing her letters telling her how I felt. I spent several nights in her dorm room, but she didn't respond to my advances, even when we slept in the same bed. Finally she explained to me that she was seeing a guy named Mike and that she only liked me as a friend.

Rejected, I stopped pursuing Leanna and continued getting high and partying. My feelings for her didn't go away, but something else soon grabbed my attention. A girl from school convinced me to go to a church called the Jesus People Church. I was reluctant to go at first, but I finally agreed. It was a decision that changed my life forever.

The first day that I went to the Jesus People Church, a man named Daniel Warren was preaching. He spoke about God's love and mankind's need for a Savior, which could be fulfilled only by believing in Jesus Christ. His words struck my heart in a way that I had never experienced before. I remember thinking that perhaps God was what I had been searching for to fill the void in my life.

When Daniel Warren offered a chance to go to the altar to pray and begin a personal relationship with God, I knew that was what I needed and so I went to the altar and received Jesus Christ into my heart as my Lord and Savior. After I prayed, I went to the back room and talked with a woman named Cassie. She explained more about what I had just done, gave me a Bible and some literature, and prayed with me.

I began attending church regularly after that day and I saw Cassie every Sunday. She was excited about my newfound faith and told me about a program called Parkhouse, where new Christians could go to learn about God and establish a biblical foundation in their lives for the years to come. I had told her that I smoked pot and cigarettes and she thought the program would help me in both my spiritual and physical life. The idea fascinated me and I began thinking seriously about it. I wanted to learn more about God and it seemed like the perfect opportunity. I had a serious decision to make, however, because I soon found out that I would have to leave school to attend because it was required for all Parkhouse students to move into the facility.

After thinking it over for a while, I decided to try living at Parkhouse. I stopped going to Concordia Bible College and moved into the girls' house. The house rules were different from what I was used to because everyone had to help with cooking and cleaning, but I adjusted and my life began to change in gradual but noticeable ways.

There was a Bible study every Thursday night and it was a rare meeting in which the room wasn't filled with people. I started waking up at six o'clock every morning to pray and I studied my Bible diligently. I became involved in many of the activities at Parkhouse, including house meetings, singing, skits, and street evangelism. I could feel myself changing for the better. When I looked in the mirror every morning, I had a glow on my face and a light in my eyes that had never been there before. I could feel the closeness of God due to my time spent in prayer and reading the Bible. I began to develop a desire to share the gospel of Jesus Christ and the good news about what He had done in my life. I grew bold when we did street evangelism in downtown Minneapolis and I began talking about the love of God to people I had never met. I didn't know it at the time, but it was God calling out to me, asking me to follow His plan for me as an evangelist.

As well as my time at Parkhouse went, there were several incidents that brought pieces of my old life crashing back. I ran into an old friend one night and, during a moment of weakness, I went back to his house with him and smoked some pot. I became disgusted with myself, however, and told one of the house parents what I had done. I repented and that was the only time I smoked pot during my stay at Parkhouse.

I also became attracted to one of the girls living at the house, a girl named Dodi. We developed a close friendship as we ministered to people in churches and nursing homes and I found myself wanting to have more than just a friendship.

Just as I had done with Leanna, I found a way to sleep in the same bed with Dodi one night. Dodi was far from comfortable with my advances and she told the house parents what had happened the very next morning. I was called into their room and they asked me to tell them about the previous night. I told them what I had done and that I had tried to make the first move.

"Why did you think it was okay to approach Dodi in that way?"

"I thought it was what she wanted, too," I told them, even though I knew that she was interested in a guy named Ronny.

"Do you know that what you did was wrong?" they asked me.

"Yeah," I answered.

After talking with the house parents for a while longer, I repented and they prayed with me. Nothing more was ever said about the incident the entire time I stayed at Parkhouse.

During one of the holidays while I was at Parkhouse, I decided to visit my family in Pennsylvania. I went home and told them everything that had been happening in my life and I shared the gospel with my mother and younger brother Mitchell, leading them both to Christ.

Before I left to return to Minneapolis, my brother Robert confided to me that he had contracted HIV. I was shocked, but he made me promise not to tell anyone else in the family. I went back to Minnesota without saying anything to my mother or siblings.

The program at Parkhouse lasted an entire year, and when my time was done in 1981, I moved out and rented the basement of a house in Richfield, Minnesota, a suburb of Minneapolis. I continued attending Jesus People Church after I moved and met a wonderful man named Laurence, a drummer in the church band and a bicyclist.

Laurence and I hit it off well and we soon started dating. I still had thoughts about being with women, but I managed to control them and didn't pursue anything. After dating for three years, Laurence and I decided to change churches and we began to attend Summit Assemblies of God in St. Paul.

I fell in love with Laurence and wanted my family to meet him. When one of my sisters had a wedding, I figured that it was the perfect opportunity to introduce Laurence to my family. I wondered if they would approve of me marrying a white man, but color didn't matter to my family; they only cared about how Laurence treated me. They adored him and were very happy that I was dating someone because they had all thought that I was going to become a lesbian.

Laurence and I were happy for quite a while. I got a job assembling computer chips at a company called Control Data and Laurence lived close enough that I could see him often. I was befriended by an older couple named the Bittermans who lived across the street from me and we spent a lot of time at their house. Mr. Bitterman helped Laurence fix my car in the garage and change the oil while Mrs. Bitterman was determined to teach me how to bake sweet potato pie.

Even with Mrs. Bitterman's cooking lessons, it was usually Laurence who prepared the food. Every Friday night, he made dinners with a lot of carbohydrates because he was a bicyclist and went on long weekend trips. He would often "carb-up" on a Friday night and ride from Minneapolis to Duluth during the weekend, a trip that takes seven hours by car. Although I tried to be encouraging, his long trips on the weekends left me lonely and looking for ways to fill the void caused by his absence.

After we had been dating for about two years, Laurence proposed. I accepted and we began our engagement. I was happier than I had ever been in my life, but it was a happiness that didn't last.

I met Laurence's immediate family and, even though the rest of the family loved me, his mother took an instant disliking to me. I was black and they were white and she didn't approve of our relationship because she thought mixed-race marriages were wrong. I remember one day, when Laurence and I helped his parents pack in order to move, his mother forced me to stay in the basement the entire time because she didn't want the rest of the family to see "the black girl" Laurence was dating.

At the same time, another problem entered my life, one that threatened to shatter my relationship with Laurence far beyond what his mother's actions could ever have hoped to accomplish. It was a problem I should have seen coming; even Laurence became aware of it and warned me, but I refused to acknowledge it or do anything about it until it was far too late.

I was working at Control Data, soldering computer chips and trying my best to live the way that God wanted me to live. I even sat alone during my lunch breaks and read my Bible, though I am sure that my coworkers wondered what I was doing. After working there for a while, a woman named Ruth began saying hello to me every time she saw me. She asked me questions during lunch about what I was reading and I tried to talk to her about spiritual things, convinced that I might be able to help her start a relationship with God.

Ruth and I developed a friendship and soon we were spending every day with each other. I lived about fifteen minutes from work and Ruth lived about forty-five minutes away, so she often came over to my house after we had finished our shift. We began spending so much time together that Laurence confronted me about it one day.

"Don't you think you're spending too much time with Ruth?" he asked.

"No," I told him, "it's just that you're gone so much all the time on your biking trips. I don't have anyone to spend time with."

But that wasn't the truth. Ruth and I had been talking about how we were becoming attracted to each other, but I told her that I couldn't do anything because I was engaged to Laurence. Despite my engagement, I still spent every moment available with Ruth when Laurence wasn't around. She even took me to meet her family. As the months passed, I found myself thinking less about Laurence and more about Ruth. I looked forward to his long bike trips because that meant I could spend more time with Ruth.

Meanwhile, our wedding plans were still moving forward. I had my wedding dress picked out, along with bridesmaids' dresses, and Laurence and I had found our wedding rings. We were also in premarital counseling with our pastor, Pastor Ted. We had decided to go to counseling so we could discuss the expectations we both had for our marriage, even though I was becoming increasingly confused about my feelings, both for Laurence and for men in general.

Finally, everything came tumbling down. I went to Ruth's house one night after work and we talked together as usual, but soon we realized that it was becoming late. Ruth asked me to spend the night. I decided that it was too late for me to go home and so I agreed and we continued talking. Our talking led to other things, however, and that night I had my first sexual encounter with a woman.

When I woke up the next morning, I knew that my life was going to change drastically because of what I had done the previous night. I had a deep feeling of shame because I knew what I had done was wrong. I couldn't feel the presence of God like I normally did. It was as if He had left me. I kept thinking that He didn't love me anymore, but my night with Ruth so dominated my thoughts that I pushed my thoughts of God away to a corner of my mind.

I knew that I no longer had feelings for Laurence because I was infatuated with Ruth and wanted to be with her all the time. I called Pastor Ted and made an appointment to meet with him that very same day. I told him everything that had happened, that my feelings for Laurence had changed, and that I had begun a relationship with Ruth. Pastor Ted told me that I needed to call off my wedding with Laurence and that I needed to seek help about what to do with the feelings I was experiencing for Ruth. I didn't get counseling for my feelings, but I did agree to call off the wedding, even though I dreaded telling Laurence what had happened.

I called Laurence later that day and told him that we had to talk. When we met, I told him everything that had happened. He was stunned.

"We can still work this out," he kept saying. Tears were running down his cheeks. "It wasn't you that did this. I know you and you're not like that. She coerced you somehow."

"No," I told him, taking the engagement ring off my finger and handing it back to him. "It was both of us. I love her, Laurence, and I want to be with her. I can't be with you anymore."

Laurence was heartbroken, but there was nothing he could do about the situation. My mind was made up. My only hope was that I never hurt anyone again the same way that I hurt him.

I realized that I couldn't be with Ruth and still hold onto everything else that was then part of my life. I knew I would have to leave my church and many of the people there behind. I felt somehow that I would want to return one day, but I needed an assurance that I would still be able to come back. I prayed and asked God for a promise. I read Matthew 16:18, which says, "On this rock I will build my church, and the gates of Hades will not overcome it."

I didn't know what that verse meant, but I tucked it away in my heart. Then, with a deep breath, I walked away from God, I walked away from church, I walked away from Laurence, and I entered the lesbian lifestyle.

Chapter 3

BAD DEALINGS

BECOMING A LESBIAN WASN'T AN INSTANTANEOUS change. I struggled with it. I'm fairly certain that Ruth had a hard time with it as well. We were each other's first same sex-partners and the adjustment to a new way of living and thinking was difficult. It was one thing to be a lesbian in private, but actually admitting it or showing it in public somehow made it more real and concrete.

There was a gay bar called Ladies' Night and Ruth wanted to go in and socialize on the weekends, but it took me a while to work up enough courage to enter. For two weekends in a row I had decided to go in, but I ended up just sitting in the car and watching the women that went in and out. I knew I wanted to go in, but I couldn't bring myself to do it. Finally, on the third weekend, I went into the bar.

It had a normal bar-like atmosphere in many ways: there was a bar area, tables, a DJ booth, a dance floor, and the basement had pool tables and dartboards. There were also things that you don't see in most bars. Sundays offered an interesting role-reversal event called "Taco Sundays," where many of the lesbian women went to the bar to eat and watch sports while the gay men would stay at home and cook for their boyfriends.

Some of the women there looked and dressed like men, but the women they were with were very feminine. I began to think about my role in my relationship with Ruth. Did I want to be the boy or the girl? I decided to play the masculine role and I began watching the other masculine lesbians for cues about how to dress, walk, talk, and treat my partner.

There were also many men dressed in drag that frequented the bar, some so well disguised that I was disappointed on several occasions when I found out that they were men. There were also times when married couples came in and the husband would ask one of us girls to come home with him and his wife. I would have loved to volunteer to go with the couples because I wanted to sleep with the wives, but I didn't want anything to do with the men, even if they just watched.

I found myself going back to some of my old habits and began smoking pot that some of the bar customers were more than happy to sell me. The bar became such a part of my life that I would work at my job and then immediately go to the bar to drink and socialize, sometimes with Ruth, but many times without her.

A strange thing began happening while I drank and talked with the people in the bar: I started talking about God. I didn't mean to do it and often didn't realize what I was saying until someone would call my attention to it.

"What are you talking about?" they would ask me.

"Oh, nothing," I always said, a little embarrassed and wondering what exactly had caused me to start preaching. Whenever this happened, I got mad at God because I felt as if He were preventing me from beginning relationships with the women at the bar. He was trying to get my attention, but I ignored Him because I was trying to have fun.

During the changes of those first few months, I told my family about my lifestyle decision. To my surprise, they accepted me and did not judge me. My mother told me that she already knew. I was relieved.

I also had the opportunity to meet Ruth's parents. They liked me as a person, but as Christians, they didn't approve of my relationship with their daughter. One day, they invited us over and tried to talk to us.

"Ruth, Janet," they said, "we need to tell you that what you are doing is wrong. It doesn't mean that we don't love either of you, but you need to turn your hearts back to God."

I tried to ignore what Ruth's parents said, but their words stuck with me. I felt guilty every time I saw them because I wanted to respect them. I didn't feel at peace. I knew that I had walked away from God, but I didn't want to give up my new lifestyle. I wanted God and I wanted to regain my peace somehow, but I wasn't willing to pay the price. It was a constant push-and-pull battle that waged inside my head and within my heart.

My inner struggle and discontent led me to start searching for a way to fill the void again. I grew bored with Ruth after a year and I wanted to find a way out of the relationship. Something in my life wasn't working and even though I knew I needed to make my heart right with God, I tried to blame my troubles on Ruth. I spent more time at the bar without her and eventually met another woman named Linda.

Linda was very feminine and all the girls wanted her. She dressed in skirts and wore pumps, far different from the way I looked. I was considered one of the boys because of how I acted and dressed, but I didn't want to be with someone similar to me. I wanted someone like Linda.

Linda and I got along well and soon I was dating both her and Ruth at the same time. Neither knew about the other, but I knew that I couldn't keep seeing them both and so I tried to break up with Ruth.

"Your parents are making too much of a fuss about us," I told her. "I think it would be better if we didn't see each other anymore."

Even with my excuses, Ruth and I didn't break up right away. She was so crushed and upset that we continued seeing each other for a while because I didn't want to hurt her. Eventually, however, we were able to part ways. Meanwhile, I kept dating Linda. She took me to meet some of her family and we continued hanging out at the bar.

One night, while Linda and I were at the bar, a man named Andy approached us. Andy seemed to be a nice guy as we began talking with him.

"Do you girls want to make some money?" Andy asked us after a while.

"Sure," Linda said, "what do you have in mind?"

"Follow me outside," he told us.

We walked out of the bar and Andy handed Linda a bag of cocaine and a phone number to call.

"Sell this," he said. "You can even take some of it for yourself, if you want. If you need more, just call that number."

I nodded, but then asked, "How will she know who to sell it to?"

Andy grinned. "Don't worry. They will come to you."

Linda and I both tried the cocaine and I decided that I wanted to make money as well. Andy was right, the customers did come. Word of mouth spread quickly and soon I had people calling me at all hours of the night, needing to get high. After several months, I was making a lot of money as a cocaine dealer. I started using the coke myself and soon I was addicted to it as well. I also started smoking cigarettes again as a side habit.

I did a lot of my dealing at Ladies Night. I began to get a lot of customers and was always looking for ways to expand my market. I grew bolder selling the cocaine and even brought it into my workplace. I spent almost as much time at work dealing drugs as I did soldering computer chips.

If I ran out of coke, I called Andy and gave him money to get me more. We met face to face sometimes, but he also sent a girl named Victoria to make deliveries. Linda and I both had a crush on Victoria so we were always happy when she dropped off the drugs or picked up money.

No matter who brought the drugs, Andy always made sure they came. We found out that his nice-guy personality from the first night we met was only an act. He had a mean streak and we discovered that he was a pimp in addition to being a drug dealer. I didn't care, though, because I was making money and I thought I was happy. My position as a dealer gave me a certain status and power with those to whom I sold and it seemed as if I was gaining more friends than ever, even though they only befriended me for the drugs I sold.

I left some cocaine in the freezer at my apartment one night before I went to work. It was all gone when I came home, about five hundred dollars worth. I panicked and began ripping through the apartment, trying to find out what had happened to it. I called the apartment manager and he said that he had let a girl into the apartment while I had been at work. When I talked to Linda, however, she said she had no idea what I was talking about.

I knew that I had to call Andy and tell him what had happened, but I dreaded doing it. It was like I was living through a nightmare. I called him and he came over to my apartment with Victoria.

As soon as he heard that I had lost the cocaine, Andy pulled a gun out of his jacket, cocked it, and put it to my head.

I was scared to death. I didn't dare move.

"You'd better get me my money," he threatened, "or I will kill you. Come up with it quickly because you don't have very much time."

I was shaking after Andy left. I didn't know what to do. I didn't have the money and I didn't want to ask him for more drugs to sell until I paid him back.

I finally decided to take the apartment complex to conciliation court. My name was the only name on the lease and I told the judge that the manager had let someone else into my apartment without my permission and that they had stolen five hundred dollars. The manager tried to argue that my "money" had actually been cocaine, but once the judge heard that my name was the only name on the lease and that the manager had let a stranger into my apartment, he sided with me. I won the case and quickly paid Andy the five hundred dollars.

My drug addiction continued despite my close encounter with death. Cocaine was fun and, to all appearances, I was having a great time getting high every day. Even though I smiled at the people around me, I was miserable inside. I felt lost and disgusted with myself, knowing that I needed to do something different, but not willing to do what was necessary. God was still there, calling me, tugging at the back of my mind and on the corner of my heart. I told myself that I wasn't ready to go back to God so I did my best to ignore Him.

Linda and I eventually moved to southern Minneapolis, looking for new ways to support our drug addiction. We rented a corner apartment and spent our evenings getting high on cocaine and playing Rummy Five Hundred.

Linda started a new job at a photo development store, hoping for a steady income and another place to sell drugs. She quickly figured out how to steal money from the company by developing photos and giving them to the customers without ringing the transaction through the cash register. She pocketed all the money she received. She became so good at it that one night she brought home more than one thousand dollars. We used the money she stole to buy even more drugs.

My cocaine addiction started having serious effects on my body, especially combined with the eating disorder I had developed. I had become bulimic, purging my food and afraid to let myself eat because I didn't want to have the weight problems with which other members of my family struggled. The combination of the coke and bulimia affected my vision, leaving me unable to see anything but blackness on more than one occasion.

Linda had to call the hospital at least five separate times because I told her that I had lost my vision. The ambulance rushed me to the hospital and the hospital told me that I needed to start treatment for my drug addiction and my bulimia. I always put the doctors off, telling them that I would begin treatment the next day, knowing that I would only go back to my cocaine instead of getting help. As much as I tried to deny it, however, I knew I needed help. I told God that if He let me live, I would go back to Him. If only I would have done it sooner.

I continued dealing drugs, but things were getting out of control. I was constantly getting into fights because I had discovered ways to rip people off when I sold the cocaine. I started skimming a little bit off the top of each order, thinking I would be able to get away with it, but people noticed and I soon had a number of people who wanted to kill me. It didn't take much for me to avoid paying my bills and so bill collectors also began looking for me.

I was laid off from my job so I applied to work at Ford Motor Company and was soon called back for an interview. I passed the interview and a dexterity test with flying colors, but when I was told that I had to give a urine sample, I got worried. I had a friend urinate into a cup for me and I passed her urine off as my own when I went to get tested.

My trick worked and I was hired to put clips onto gas tanks, but it didn't take long for my job at Ford to go poorly as well. My coworkers and I worked high most of the time, snorting cocaine and smoking pot on our lunch breaks or in the bathroom. After working there for six months, I developed carpal tunnel syndrome in my hands and it became too painful to continue working. After I was put on workman's compensation, I poured even more effort into selling drugs.

I began hanging out with Ruth again because I suspected that Linda had been cheating on me, even though I couldn't prove it. I was with Ruth one night and we stopped by my apartment to get some clothes when I found Linda with another girl in our bed. I was high at the time and became furious, kicking both Linda and the girl while they were on the bed. I knew that I would completely lose my temper if I stayed any longer so I had Ruth take me away until I had cooled down enough to move my things out of the apartment. My heart was broken to the point where I didn't want to live anymore.

I found another apartment across town and lived by myself for several months, but my life didn't improve at all.

Ruth saw how far I had fallen and tried to put me into treatment for my drug addiction, but I walked out after a day. I wasn't ready. I didn't want to change my life for anyone else. If I was going to do it, it had to be for me.

On my thirtieth birthday, as I lay on my couch smoking crack, I remember wondering what had happened to my life. I was utterly miserable. I was dealing and doing drugs. I couldn't seem to maintain a relationship. I was unable to work an honest job. I could feel God gently tugging on my heart—but I just wasn't quite sure what to do about it.

Finally, I placed a call to Ford Motor Company's counseling hotline and told the counselor that I was on workman's compensation and that I was struggling with a drug addiction and needed help. The counselor told me to come in to the clinic and that same day I started treatment at Fairview Southdale Hospital. I told God that if He would help me overcome my drug addiction, I would never go back to cocaine again.

Chapter 4

FIGHTING ADDICTIONS

I BEGAN LEARNING THAT GOD'S LOVE IS GENUINE AS HE helped take away my cocaine addiction in 1989, even though I was still far from completely giving my life over to Him. God gives grace, however, and it is both sweet and amazing. I have been drug-free ever since I entered treatment all those years ago.

I spent two weeks in treatment at Fairview Southdale Hospital. I told the doctors and counselors everything about my drug addiction and my bulimia.

"We'll help you take care of it," they promised me. "First, we're going to take care of your cocaine addiction and then we'll get your bulimia under control."

They did help me. As I came down off the cocaine, I began experiencing withdrawals. I was put on anti-depressants for a while to help me deal with my body's craving for cocaine. The doctors also made sure that I ate enough food to keep myself healthy. After every meal, a nurse sat in the hallway with me for an hour so I couldn't force my food back up by purging.

I began meeting with a counselor and told her about other parts of my life.

"Not only am I a crack addict and bulimic, but I'm also living a lesbian lifestyle," I confessed to her, partially to see how she would react and partially to see if she could help me find a way out. "I know my homosexuality is wrong in God's eyes, but I don't know what to do about it."

"Don't worry about that, Janet," she told me.

"But it's wrong."

"No, it's not wrong, it's just a choice to live a different way than most people," she answered.

Every counselor I met told me the same thing about my lesbianism, but their words didn't sit well deep within my heart. As much as I wanted to believe homosexuality was only one of several moral choices, an inner voice kept telling me that the way I had been living was wrong. There was constant war inside me.

When I came out of treatment at Fairview, I immediately joined an Alcoholics Anonymous group. I wasn't an alcoholic, but I figured that an addiction was an addiction and I was determined not to go back to cocaine. Over the next ninety days, I went to ninety AA meetings and I was able to stay away from cocaine.

I began thinking clearly for the first time during those three months of meetings. It had been years since I had been clean of drugs and I began to hear God's calling on my life again. He was tugging me back toward church, putting people and things into my life that drew me to Him.

I wasn't ready to leave the lesbian lifestyle, but I decided to start going to a church called Bethlehem Baptist. I attended irregularly, dabbling with one foot in the church lifestyle and one foot in the homosexual community. I tried evangelism by handing out gospel tracts to strangers on the bus, but I also found myself spending a lot of time in lesbian bars.

I wasn't in a relationship during that time because my counselors told me that any romantic involvements within a year of recovering from an addiction could take the place of the addiction itself. I was too afraid of returning to my cocaine habit to take any chances with a relationship, but my fear didn't stop me from going back to the homosexual community.

I was searching for something. I felt as if healing and restoration for my life were just out of my reach and I was desperate for them. I knew I needed God and so if I saw someone walking down the street, carrying what I thought was a Bible, I literally ran after them.

"Hey, you're a Christian, aren't you?" I would ask. "I'm a Christian too, but I've backslidden. I'm living a lesbian lifestyle."

I tried to be honest about the way I was living my life with everyone I met, as if I thought honesty could serve as a substitute for repentance. I figured that if someone knew who I was and what I was doing when they first met me, they could accept me or reject me right away. If someone was going to eventually reject me, I wanted them to do it immediately so I didn't have to be hurt after I came to know them.

I met one young couple at Bethlehem Baptist who not only accepted me, but also began helping me recover from my destructive living habits. Lucy and her husband John began teaching me how to manage my finances. I had avoided paying bills all throughout my drug dealing days and I had no idea how to even balance a checkbook. They kept my checkbook for me and taught me how to keep track of my money. They were so kind to me. When John saw that I was driving a car with no heat in the middle of a cold Minnesota winter, he and Lucy decided to loan me money to buy a new car.

Despite the kindness of Lucy and John in teaching me about money, they weren't able to help me with all my issues. I still struggled with bulimia. It got out of control again and it became so bad that I began having double vision. I finally decided to go to a hospital in the area and the doctor there told me that I was dehydrated and that my electrolytes were out of balance. I stayed in the hospital for several days and remember having the nurses tape the toilet seat shut so that I couldn't purge after I ate.

I was released after treatment, but the hospital staff referred me to a program for overcoming bulimia through the University of Minnesota. I enrolled myself in the program and began going after work, but it wasn't enough to keep another struggle out of my life.

I started working at Control Data for a second time, which brought me back to a steady interaction with Ruth. Even though I was no longer romantically interested in her, I tried to renew our former relationship. I wanted so desperately to be loved by someone, to be with someone who cared about me that it didn't matter to me that she only thought of me as a friend.

I stopped going to Bethlehem Baptist because I didn't want to play around with God by living two different lives. I kept in touch with Lucy and John, and I knew that they were praying for me, but we gradually drifted apart. The thought of not living a double life consumed me. I wasn't ready to leave the lesbian lifestyle, but I was afraid of what might happen to me if I didn't. Sometimes I became so terrified that I couldn't go to sleep at night because I didn't want to die before I had the opportunity to return to God.

My new relationship with Ruth never went beyond friendship because she wasn't as interested in me as she had been in the past and because my fear kept me from following through with it. I still spent a lot of time with her, however, and through Ruth, I came into contact with more trouble when she introduced me to some of her roommate's friends.

Lena and her boyfriend Carter were cocaine dealers and I quickly befriended them, pushing all my past experiences with the world of drugs to the back of my mind. After knowing them for several weeks, Lena asked if they could keep some of their cocaine at my apartment. I said yes and gave Lena a key and she stored it in my closet. Lena came and went as she pleased while I went to work and attended the bulimia program at the University of Minnesota.

I didn't use the cocaine, but I sometimes stole a little and sold it when I needed extra money. Lena never mentioned anything about it, however, so I don't think she ever noticed that some of the cocaine was missing. She trusted me and thought I was an honest and good girl.

One day, after several months of storing their drugs in my closet, Lena, Carter, and another girl tried to make a deal on the street. They were going to sell four ounces of cocaine to a client, but when they arrived and began the deal, they found out that their "client" was actually an undercover police officer. All three of them were arrested and the girl with Lena and Carter began talking to the police, telling them that all of the drugs were stored in my apartment.

When I came home from the bar at about one o'clock in the morning, I found my door torn off the hinges and lying on the floor. My apartment was ransacked and I was sure that someone had broken in to rob me.

I panicked and immediately tried to contact Lena and Carter, but wasn't able to reach anyone. I drove to their house and knocked on the door, but no one was there. When I looked through the window, their house looked as if it had been ransacked just like my apartment. Finally, I went to Lena's sister's house and she told me what had happened. While I was talking to her sister, Lena called from jail.

"Don't worry, Janet," Lena told me, "we're going to protect you. Just make sure that you tell the police that you didn't know anything about what was going on."

I agreed to do what she told me and spent the night at her sister's house. The next day I called the manager of the apartment complex and told him that my apartment had been broken into and that the door needed to be fixed. Then I called the police, and when I found out there was a warrant out for my arrest, I told them that I was turning myself in.

I went to the police station and turned myself into the custody of an officer named John Booker. As he led me into a room to be questioned, I was convinced that I was going to end up in jail for a long time.

"Well, Janet, were you a part of all this?" he asked, referring to the drug ring.

"No," I told him. "I don't know anything about it."

"Do you know that we found a lot of cocaine and money in the closet of your apartment?"

"Lena and Carter were my friends," I said. "They just told me that they were going to keep some money in my closet. I never looked in their bag; I didn't know they had cocaine in it, too."

Officer Booker stared at me for a while before he finally shook his head. "What is a girl like you doing mixed up with people like this? You seem like a good person. When we were searching through your apartment, we found Bibles and Christian books everywhere. The drugs just don't seem to fit in with everything else we found at your place."

To my surprise and relief, the police believed me and decided to let me go. I went home and immediately began cleaning my apartment, determined never to get caught up in drugs again. I tried to go on living my normal life. That was when I met Nina.

I was still attending Alcoholics Anonymous every week and during the course of our meetings, I came to know Nina. Nina was married and had three children, but her marriage was falling apart because she had problems with both alcohol and gambling. We talked during the meetings, formed a friendship, and then began spending time together outside of the program. It didn't take very long before the relationship turned sexual.

Nina had had a number of affairs, but I was the first woman with whom she had ever cheated on her husband. I was worried that she might have some sexually transmitted diseases from all of her relationships and so I asked her to take an HIV test. When she tested negative, I felt more at ease and we continued our affair.

As our relationship progressed, Nina brought me to her house to meet her husband and children, none of whom had any idea about what their mother was doing with me. Nina wanted to tell her husband about our affair, but it took her a long time to figure out how to break the news. When she finally did tell him, she separated from her husband and we moved into a townhouse together in a town called Maple Grove. She was able to obtain custody of two of her children and so Laura and Jenna moved in with us as well. Suddenly, for the first time since I had left home, I was part of a family again.

We tried hard to make our family work. Even though Nina made much more money than I did, I became convinced that it was my job to provide for the household by putting food on the table. I worked harder than ever and settled in to the masculine role while Nina became the feminine partner.

I got along fairly well with Nina's girls, even though I was more of a disciplinarian than she was. The girls hated cleaning and I had to bribe them in order to get them to clean their rooms. When Nina and I first began our relationship, the girls always ran to her, but she made them listen to me as well and soon the girls treated me like another parent. It seemed as if everything was going to work out. I had dreams of our non-traditional family being like *Little House on the Prairie*, where everyone loved each other and all the problems were worked out by the end of every episode.

Life went well for the first few months of the relationship. Both Nina and I spent our time working and taking care of the kids and, at times, it seemed like a normal life. We even talked about God together. I tried to convince Nina that she needed God and even told her that I would one day return to Him.

"I feel like what I'm doing with you is wrong," I confessed to her during one of our conversations about God. "I feel like God doesn't approve of our relationship."

"Well, why don't you go back to Him now?" she asked. "What are you waiting for?"

"I'm not ready yet," I admitted.

Even though I was reluctant to turn back to God, I still lived in fear of the consequences if I didn't. I was still afraid on many nights that I would die before I had a chance to make my life right with God. My conversations with Nina helped because she seemed to genuinely listen, but talking with her was no substitute for obeying the calling I felt on my heart. I tried to ignore God's call for just a little longer, but my carefully constructed family life soon began falling apart.

I had taken up the new hobby of working out at a gym because the Alcoholics Anonymous program taught that if you subtracted something as strong as an addiction in your life, you needed to replace it with something healthy. Exercise became my substitution for cocaine.

In addition to exercising, I became fascinated with the idea of bodybuilding. I worked out with the goal of entering a contest and finally got to a level of fitness that I thought would allow me to enter a competition. I looked around and finally found a bodybuilding competition close by and entered my name.

When the time came for the competition, I was both excited and nervous. It was in Rochester, about two hours from where we were living at the time, and Nina and I were going to drive down together. Nina never came home that night. I called everywhere, finally finding her at a friend's house, too drunk to drive home. She told me she would meet me at the contest so I drove to Rochester by myself.

I took first prize in the competition, but Nina didn't come until a friend dropped her off after the contest was already over. I became furious with her.

"This was my first competition," I yelled at her, "and you couldn't even show up? Do you have any idea how much this meant to me? And you didn't come because you were *drunk*?" It was the same pain, all over again, that I had suffered with my mother during my childhood.

We argued for a long time that night, but even after we made up, the situation didn't get any better. Nina began drinking and gambling regularly again and the problem grew worse, to the point where she drank so much that she blacked out.

Our relationship started spiraling downward. Nina lied to me about everything and I never knew where she had been or with whom. She came home drunk late at night, if she even came home at all. I found myself going out to look for her in bars and clubs and if I found her with anyone, man or woman, I started an argument with that person. The arguments usually ended with Nina staying at the bar while I went back home to be with her children.

I realized that my life was becoming like my mother's. I was going out to look for Nina just like my mother had gone out to look for gus. We even got into fistfights some nights when Nina came home drunk. I tried calling my mother for her advice, but soon realized that there was nothing she could do or say that was going to help me.

Nina gambled when she wasn't at the bar drinking, though I'm sure that she drank at the casinos as well. She would drive several hours to Mystic Lake Casino and gamble for days at a time. I often had no idea where she had gone and I was left at home with Laura and Jenna while Nina gambled away her paycheck and our rent for the month.

from her gambling sprees, we argued for hours at a time, sometimes in front of her girls. The girls cried a lot when they saw us argue because they were only seven- and eight-years-old and our arguments sometimes turned physical. I was skinny and still had trouble with binge eating and purging, but I felt that my battle with bulimia was far better than Nina's drinking and gambling and I told her as much. Our relationship was slowly reaching a boiling point.

Things finally came to a head after we moved again. Interest rates were low and I decided to buy a house in Maple Grove. Nina and the girls moved with me, but not long after, Nina and I got into another fight. She told me that her late nights at the bars had begun turning into affairs. When she told me she had been cheating on me, I began beating her. I could feel my past creeping back and I decided that enough was enough.

"Get out," I screamed. "Get out! It's over!"

When she saw that I was serious, Nina packed up her things, took the girls, and got an apartment about a mile away.

Suddenly, my whole world was gone.

It didn't take very long before I fell back into depression. I tried for a while to get Nina back, but she started another relationship within a week of moving out and wouldn't even talk to me. I began going back to the gay bars every night and soon felt like I was living in them.

I hated being alone and wanted so badly to be in a relationship, but it never seemed to work. I couldn't even find comfort in reading my Bible. Every time I opened it, I could find nothing there to help me. I was miserable—a prodigal with nowhere to go.

"Help me," I finally cried out. "Please God, just take me back."

Chapter 5

GROCERY STORE ENCOUNTER

I MET HALEY IN A BAR IN 1993, NOT LONG AFTER I HAD ended my relationship with Nina. I was still holding on to my lifestyle, determined to try to make it work one last time. Haley and I exchanged phone numbers and I called her not long afterward to see if she wanted to go on a date with me. We went to a movie and enjoyed each other's company, so I called her and asked if she would see me again. We began dating regularly from that point forward, working out together and spending time at each other's houses.

Haley's roommate and I didn't get along very well. She didn't like me because I was black and she was afraid that I would steal things out of their house. She and Haley had an emergency key hidden so they could get into their house if they forgot their key, but Haley's roommate took the key away when she realized I knew its location. Because her roommate and I constantly fought, Haley decided to move in with me after four months of dating.

I fell in love with Haley because she was sweet, kind, and beautiful inside and out, but her beauty caused a few problems in our relationship. Neither of us was very confident in our sexuality and we both questioned it at times, even to each other. Because I knew that Haley was unsure about herself and also because of her looks, I became very jealous and protective if guys gave her attention. After my recent relationships, I wasn't sure that I could allow myself to trust Haley not to cheat on me.

I had problems that made life difficult for Haley as well. I was a perfectionist and I liked my house to be so clean that it looked as if no one lived there—another lingering side effect of my mother's controlling ways when I was a child. My perfectionism drove Haley crazy; she hated it. I liked Haley's parents when first introduced to them, but I didn't want them to visit very often because I was afraid they were going to make a mess in our house. I remember yelling at her dad more than once when he accidentally dropped something on our floor.

Haley and I were determined to make our relationship work, even with all of our problems. My mother and aunt came to visit for a while and Haley's mother came over to meet my family. We all ate meals together and it was as if we were trying to create a heterosexual family atmosphere while remaining in the homosexual lifestyle. We tried, but it wasn't working for me. I began feeling miserable again and grew even more restless.

I could feel God calling out to me again, whispering in my heart to come back to Him, back into His arms, and back into His sanctuary. Haley and I often drove past a church called Maple Grove Assembly of God. One day I pointed it out to her.

"Do you see that church there, Haley? I'm going to go there someday."

She gave me a confused look. "What are you talking about? Why don't you just go this Sunday?"

The thought of going so soon scared me and I tried to stall for more time. I knew God was waiting for me with open arms, but I wasn't ready or willing to fall into them just yet.

"No," I told Haley, "I'm not going to go this Sunday, but I will go there someday."

After that car ride, however, I talked a lot about going to Maple Grove Assembly of God. Haley always encouraged me to go, hoping that it would make me happy, but I always put her off saying that I would go sometime in the future.

I talked about the future a lot with Haley, but the future we imagined was far from the reality we were living. We found ourselves having discussions about our sexuality and about wanting to be with men. We both wanted to marry a man someday and have families with children, but our relationship with each other prevented either from happening. If anything, our conversations made us question our sexual identities even more.

We were so desperate to make our relationship and our dreams come together that Haley and I began talking about a surgery that would turn me into a man. I had heard about a special operation from some of my friends and even though I didn't know anyone who had had the operation, I started considering it as an option. I was scared to take such a big step, however, so we decided to seek counseling about our relationship.

Haley's mother was a devout Catholic and because of her advice, we made an appointment to see a priest at the Basilica in Minneapolis. As we began talking with him in his office, we noticed that the priest was very feminine and we guessed that he was probably gay. We told him about how Haley's parents were displeased with our lifestyle choice and about how we both eventually wanted to marry men, but we also wanted to make things work with each other. I told him that I was scared about the consequences of our lifestyle and that I couldn't go to bed some nights because I was so afraid.

What we were really looking for was for the priest to tell us whether or not what we were doing was wrong.

"Don't worry anymore," the priest told us as our session ended, "you aren't doing anything wrong. After talking with you both and seeing how much you love each other, I believe that there is no sin in the way you are choosing to live your lives."

We left the Basilica feeling validated in our lifestyle and I was less afraid that I was going to go to hell for being a lesbian. We went on with our lives the way we had before. We didn't tell others that we were a lesbian couple, but most people were able to figure it out. I brought Haley to company Christmas parties. I still tried to act masculine, keeping my hair short and dressing like a man. Deep down inside, I still knew and felt that what I was doing was wrong and that God disapproved of the way I was living.

I considered the sex-change operation more seriously after that, thinking that it might be less sinful somehow if Haley and I were more like a heterosexual couple sexually. I was afraid that I wouldn't be able to change back into a woman after the surgery. I decided not to have the operation because of the potential consequences. God had made me a woman for a reason and I wanted to return to Him someday, but I didn't think I could do that as a man.

Haley and I decided that we wanted to get married. We went to a local jewelry store and bought beautiful diamond rings for $1,500 apiece. Because getting married wasn't legally an option available to us, we committed to each other, pledging, "Until death do us part."

Again I felt God speaking to my heart, this time telling me that things in my life were about to change. I felt He was telling me that He was going to use my story in a book to help people, but the very idea of that made me laugh. I didn't think I had a story worth telling and the only thing I could think of was that a book about my life would be about coming out of drugs. I told Haley that I was going to write a book someday and she laughed as well.

Once again, however, God's calling made me feel uncomfortable. It was shedding light on how unhappy I was and it showed me that there was a better way to live if only I would turn back to Him. I could only serve one master and the master I had chosen was making me miserable.

Even though we pretended as best we could, I wasn't at all happy in my relationship with Haley. I was irritable. I had thought things would go better than they were going after we gave each other commitment rings, but we fought even more often. I began to convince myself that perhaps I wasn't in love with Haley after all.

I started having affairs, cheating on Haley while she was at work at night. I had an affair with a woman at a party, which Haley found out about. When she confronted me about it, I promised I would stop, but immediately broke my promise by being with a woman a little while later. I was getting out of control, grasping at straws. I desperately wanted something real and when I discovered that Haley couldn't give it to me, I tried to find it in other women.

Everywhere I turned and everything I tried was empty and void. I had switched jobs because a company had offered to pay me more money, but two weeks after I started, they fired me because they claimed I was trying to steal their business. Haley offered to take care of me, but I was independent and hated the idea of her supporting me financially.

When Haley had to travel out of town one week, she invited me to go with her, but I didn't want to go and told her that I needed to stay home to look for work. Instead, while she was gone, I spent more time with Carrie, a woman I met earlier. When Haley returned, she knew immediately that something was wrong. I told her that I had had another affair and that I didn't want to be in a relationship with her anymore.

I wasn't sure if I wanted any relationships at all. I had thoughts about going back to God, but I didn't want to be alone—I desperately didn't want to be alone. I spent several nights with Carrie. Because she was having problems at home, I invited both her and her daughter to live with me and they accepted.

When I broke the news to Haley that Carrie and her daughter were going to move in, Haley immediately decided to move out and began living with one of our friends. As Haley moved out and Carrie moved in, I found myself in the midst of another relationship that wasn't working. Carrie and I began fighting almost immediately; I thought she was incredibly mean.

I began my own cleaning business. The business started slowly, but eventually became successful to the point where I was cleaning twenty homes a week and had to hire about ten employees to help me keep up with the work.

I dreaded going home. I made up any excuse to keep from having to return at night, spending most of my time cleaning and working out at Lifetime Fitness. I had been living the lesbian lifestyle for fourteen years and I was utterly miserable.

God began preparing my heart for what He was about to do in my life. I often watched television in bed on Sunday nights and it seemed like every time I turned on the television on, the same preacher was preaching. I listened to almost every sermon and I later found out that his name was Joel

Osteen, now a very popular author. He preached in a way that was never demeaning and his messages were about hope, change, and God's love. His words began ministering to my heart, planting seeds of change that would soon bear fruit.

Finally, one morning in October 1998, God decided that it was time. I was cleaning the equipment after hours and, at about three o'clock in the morning, I felt I needed a break, even though I rarely left work for any reason. I went to Cub Foods, a local grocery store, and was going to buy some snacks. As I was about to enter, I saw a woman leaving the store with her arms full of groceries. For whatever reason, the sight struck me as odd.

"Hey, lady," I called out, "what on earth are you doing out at this time of the night? Don't you know that you could get robbed carrying around all those groceries?"

I startled her a little. But she smiled at me and said, "I just got done dropping my son off at college and I decided to do a little shopping before I went home. My husband and I are going on a vacation and I had to get some food for our boys to eat before we leave."

"What kind of college is open until three in the morning?" I asked.

"Oh, my son goes to North Central Bible College in Minneapolis."

"North Central? I thought about going there years ago. Are you a Christian?"

"Yes, I am," she told me.

"So am I," I said. "Well," I continued—*confessed*—"I'm a backslidden Christian. I was saved at the Jesus People Church almost twenty years ago, but I've fallen into sin and haven't gone to church in a long time. But God is always sending people to tell me that He loves me."

"That's great," she said, "But you need to love Him back. Look what He has done for me."

She pulled out a letter she had written for the girls in her youth group, telling about how God had been working in her life. As I looked at the letter, I saw that it said Maple Grove Assembly of God on the letterhead. I knew then that our meeting wasn't just a coincidence.

"I know that church," I said, tapping on the letter. "I drive by it almost every day and God even told me that I was going to go there someday."

"Would you like to come with me?" she asked. "My husband and I are going to be gone for the next two weeks, but when we come back, you're welcome to come with us."

I told her that I would be willing to go and we exchanged numbers and talked for a little while longer. I found out that her name was Tami Brown and I told her how I had been living a lesbian lifestyle for the last fourteen years. I wanted to be honest with her about who I was and what I had done. As we left each other that morning, I promised to call her when she got back.

Two weeks later, I called her and I went to church for the first time since I had gone to Bethlehem Baptist. Tami and her husband introduced me to several people from the church. I told every person I met that day that I was living in a lesbian lifestyle, but they all welcomed me with open arms anyway. I felt like I had come home.

After years of misery, I felt my first glimmers of peace that day. God had sought me out—He had called me out— and I had finally listened.

Chapter 6
RESTORING FREEDOM

W HAT ARE YOU DOING ON TUESDAY NIGHTS, JANET?"
Tami Brown asked me two weeks after I started
going to church.

"I usually work doing my cleaning business," I answered.
"Why?"

"There is a women's Bible study at church for ten women
and we have one spot open. Would you like to be a part of
it?"

"I can probably arrange my work so I can clean afterward. Sure, I'll go."

The Bible study was held in the office of Pastor Gary
Hinkle at Maple Grove Assembly of God, although he didn't
attend. Two women named Jenny and Kate led the study and
had us all introduce ourselves to each other. I remember not
being able to look up from the floor as each woman told a
little about herself. I was filled with shame at the way I had
been living and because of what I had done. I just stared at my
feet, knowing that I was living a lifestyle that was wrong.

When my turn came to introduce myself, I had trouble
speaking. I wanted to be as transparent and honest as I could,
but I was disgusted with myself.

"My name is Janet Boynes," I said. "I've been living as a
lesbian for the past fourteen years, but I believe that God is
calling me out of that lifestyle. I have a desire to serve God

with my life, but I need help. If you all can help me, I will serve God."

Those women did help me and my heart began to change. I continued going to church and to Bible study every week, and Jenny and Kate ministered to me as often as they were able. They encouraged me to call them several times during the week as an accountability check and they both always seemed to be there when I needed them.

I was still living with Carrie, but my experiences at church severely strained our relationship. Like so many of my past relationships, Carrie and I began arguing heavily about everything. This time was different, however. Instead of seeking to fill the void caused by our failing relationship with yet another affair, I filled it with Bible verses, prayer, and time at church. Filling my life with the things of God made a huge difference in my life. Even though I was upset about Carrie, our fighting didn't send me into a tailspin like it had in the past.

Carrie and I began sleeping on different floors and she began staying out late at night. Our sexual relationship was mostly over, but we were tightly involved emotionally. We still went out to dinner together and I sometimes brought her daughter to church with me. It was a difficult time for me because I was caught in a transition between two completely different worlds—the life I had lived in misery for the past fourteen years and the new life God was calling me to live through the ministry of Maple Grove Assembly of God and the women's Bible study I was attending.

I knew that God had something planned for my life. Two nights in a row I had visions of myself preaching and sharing my testimony in front of thousands of people. I was still cleaning houses and I began to practice preaching in the mirror with a broom handle as my microphone.

During this time, God kept tugging on my heart about sharing what had happened to me with others. He directed me to Bible verses that I could share and I also had a vision of talking to my pastor in his office about speaking. When I told Jenny and Kate about it, they encouraged me to talk with Pastor Gary. I prayed about everything for several weeks and then decided to make an appointment with Pastor Gary.

I brought my diaries to show Pastor Gary what God had been putting on my heart. After I finished telling him everything, he leaned back in his chair and smiled.

"What do you think about May 2?" he asked.

"What about May 2?" I asked in return, not quite sure what he meant.

"Would you like to share your testimony then?"

"Do you mean that night?"

"Nope." His grin grew wider. "I mean during the first service on Sunday morning."

"You really want me to speak on Sunday morning?" I couldn't believe it.

"Yes, Janet, I think you should."

"Okay, I'll do it." I wasn't sure if Pastor Gary knew what he was getting himself into. I didn't know if *I* knew what I was getting myself into. Even though I had two months to prepare, I started working on my message right away. I carefully wrote out my testimony and everything that I was going to say and got it approved by Pastor Gary.

I invited Carrie to come and listen to me speak, but she absolutely refused. Even though we still talked to each other, she didn't want to hear anything more from me about leaving the homosexual lifestyle, especially not in the middle of a church.

I was excited about speaking and I asked a woman from our church to help me pick out a feminine suit to wear when I spoke because I didn't have any idea about how to buy women's clothes.

The morning of May 2 came quicker than I thought it would. After the praise and worship part of the service was over, I went up to the pulpit and began to share my story and explain how God's grace and love had called me out of homosexuality. When I finished speaking, Pastor Gary gave an invitation for those who had loved ones struggling with homosexuality to come forward to the altar for prayer. When more than thirty people came forward, I thanked God in my heart that I had chosen to obey His calling to share my testimony of His love.

A week after I spoke at church, I received a telephone call from home. My biological father had died. I struggled over whether or not I should return home for his funeral because he had never taken an active interest in my life. Finally, I decided I should go. I took a flight to Philadelphia and saw some of my family and friends for the first time in years. As I reunited with them, I told them what God had been doing in my life. I even handed out tapes that had been made of me giving my testimony in church. People were amazed at the change in me.

When I returned, Jenny, one of the leaders of the women's Bible study I attended, called me and told me that I needed to have Carrie move out in order to be accountable because people were going to be looking at my life as an example. I asked Carrie to move out, but it didn't completely end our relationship. We still saw each other and she tried to get me to sleep with her again. There were times when her advances made it hard for me because the temptation was strong to go back to homosexuality, but I didn't give in. I was open and honest with the women from my Bible study and they kept me accountable. I prayed, I read Scripture and Christian books that talked about resisting temptation, and I listened to audio tapes filled with sermons, Scripture, and songs. Through it all, God gave me the strength to keep from falling back into a sexual relationship with Carrie.

My life then took a turn in a new direction. Jenny invited me to live with her and her husband and their family. She knew that I was still tempted to go back to Carrie and she wanted to give me an opportunity for more accountability after having given my testimony.

I really didn't know what to think about her offer. I was a forty-year-old woman who had lived on her own for more than half her life. I had no idea how I would adapt to leaving my own house to live with a family, living by their rules and their way of life. The thought of becoming dependent like that again didn't appeal to me very much, but I knew I needed that accountability. I desperately wanted to do what was right in the eyes of God, and I was afraid that if I stayed by myself, I would stumble and fall back into the lifestyle I had just left. I prayed long and hard about what decision I should make. Finally, I decided to do it.

I quickly sold my house and moved in with Jenny and her family. It was tough and I experienced some culture shock because of my new environment. There were house rules that had to be followed and expectations that I had to live up to, even though I was a grown woman. I was expected to be at the family dinners and to participate in the family devotions. I saw everything, good and bad. I saw how Jenny's family lived and worked and played and fought together. I also saw how they prayed together and how they loved each other. All of it was foreign to me because it was nothing like the childhood experiences I had growing up.

Living in Jenny's house was like a second childhood for me and there were definitely growing pains. When Jenny found out that Carrie and I still talked to each other on the phone, she told me flat out that I couldn't talk to her anymore.

"You have to leave those things behind, Janet," she told me. "Otherwise, you're going to fall back into temptation and maybe even back into homosexuality."

I didn't want to stop calling Carrie, even though I knew that Jenny was right.

It was a battle we fought over and over again. Carrie and I were still emotionally involved and, even though I had left the sexual relationship behind, I didn't want to abandon the emotional bond that I still felt with her. The emotional bond was far stronger than the sexual because I thought that she was still able to fulfill my needs. I knew what Jenny expected of me, but I wasn't ready or willing to live up to those expectations just yet. I kept sneaking calls to Carrie. I sometimes admitted it when Jenny asked me if I had talked to Carrie, but other days I lied to Jenny because I was afraid of getting kicked out of her house.

While Jenny and I were fighting over my desire to talk with Carrie, something else happened that broke my heart. I received a call at two o'clock one morning from my mother. My brother Robert was in the hospital, dying from full-blown AIDS. My mother told me to come as quickly as I could to Philadelphia and so I made reservations for the first flight out of Minneapolis, but it didn't leave until later that morning. Later that morning proved to be too late. Two hours after her first call, my mother called again saying that Robert had died.

When I finally made it to Philadelphia, I found out the whole story, a horror I'm glad I didn't witness.

Robert had been in prison for selling cocaine and when the AIDS virus reached its final stage, it began shutting down his organs one by one. Even though he had told me about being infected with HIV years earlier, he had never told the rest of my family about the HIV or AIDS because he didn't want them to see him suffer.

When the prison guards rushed him to the hospital at the prison, they didn't even bother to contact my family and tell them what happened. My family would never have found out about Robert being in the hospital if a fellow prisoner hadn't seen him taken in and called his mother, who in turn called my mother.

My mother and sisters rushed to the hospital, but the warden didn't want to let them in to see Robert. My brother-in-law used to work for the prison, however, and was able to convince the warden to let my mother in to see Robert. My sisters were eventually allowed to see him as well, but what they all saw would give them nightmares for years to come.

Robert was lying on the hospital gurney, still shackled, and he was bleeding everywhere. He was hemorrhaging from every orifice in his body—his eyes, his ears, his mouth, his nose, and even the pores in his skin. He was hooked up to a blood transfusion machine, but every ounce that was pumped into him bled away within minutes. My family had to put on protective clothing to even enter the room with him because he was literally sweating blood.

When the doctor came in and saw Robert still chained to his gurney, he told the guards to take the shackles off.

"Let the man die with some dignity," he said.

Robert died just a few hours later.

I cannot even imagine my family's reaction to seeing my brother like that. Even today, years later, we burst into tears whenever the subject of Robert comes up. The funeral was hard on all of us, especially when we found out that Robert had planned it in advance.

Robert's lifestyle choice before prison had kept him from talking to us very often, but he had known about his infection and had seen what eventually was coming. Some years earlier, he had bought a funeral plot for himself, his father, and my mother because he wanted to be buried in between them. His father has since joined him and one day our mother will as well.

I returned home after the funeral and immediately fell back into calling Carrie. I didn't know how to deal with my brother's death. She was a familiar voice, and I didn't feel like I had the strength to resist the temptation of talking with her. Jenny tried to intervene again, but I kept rebelling against her even though I knew she was right.

Jenny and her husband eventually took me to see Pastor Gary because they didn't know what else to do. They talked with me for a while and then they prayed for me. I could feel the struggle in my heart as part of me wanted to return to my old lifestyle and the rest of me wanted to follow God's calling on my life. I knew that I had people praying for me, Pastor Gary, Jenny and her family, and the women's Bible study. I didn't give up trying to do what was right and, even though I didn't stop talking to Carrie, I made up my mind to not lie about it to Jenny anymore.

Jenny finally put her foot down and told me that enough was enough. She said that if I called Carrie one more time, she would kick me out of her house. I knew then that she was serious and even though I didn't want to move out, I protested anyway. Jenny wouldn't listen to any of my arguments.

Carrie quickly figured out that I wasn't able to call her anymore and so she called Jenny. It was Christmas and Carrie had a gift that she wanted to bring me, but Jenny didn't want her to come to the house. She went and got the gift for me and left it outside my bedroom door.

When I found Carrie's gift, I opened it up immediately to find a small mahogany jewelry box. I stared at it for a couple minutes and then sat down on my bed and started crying. I cried because I knew that my relationship with Carrie was finally over; I cried for my brother Robert; I cried hot, bitter tears for all the changes that had happened in my life; and I cried because I didn't know what was going to happen next.

I had known since the night after I had given my testimony in church that I was being called into some sort of ministry, but I didn't know how, I didn't know where, and I had no idea what I was going to do. I knew where I had come from and I knew where I was going, but the road in between those two places was dark to me. I was scared.

With all the changes in my life, it was comforting to have people who really cared for me. Jenny and her husband Mike encouraged me and helped me build a new foundation. They helped me shape my life for the future. With their guidance, I fell into good habits for the first time in my life and began reading my Bible and praying every day.

I still couldn't believe they had invited me into their home to live with their children and be a part of their family. I learned how men and women should treat each other, the importance of spending time with your family, and about family values. I also learned how to forgive. In a very real way, my experience at Mike and Jenny's house was like a second childhood for me. It helped heal and restore me from so many of the wounds I had suffered in my first childhood.

I was like a child in a lot of other ways as well. There were many things I wasn't used to doing and hearing and so I had to struggle to adjust to them. I remember many times Jenny and her family complimented me on how I looked, but I didn't know how to respond. I wanted to return the compliment, but I felt uncomfortable doing it because I thought Jenny might misunderstand me and think I was attracted to her sexually, even though I just wanted to tell her she looked nice.

One day, I finally just blurted it out, "Jenny, I've wanted to compliment you on your looks, but I've been afraid that if I do, you'll think I want to go back to being a lesbian."

Jenny looked right back at me and said, "No, Janet, I wouldn't think that at all. When I look at you now, I see a new creation in Christ Jesus. God has been working in your life and you just aren't the same anymore."

I was a new creation, but it still wasn't always easy. I had days when I could feel my old lifestyle and habits calling out to me, but I was growing in my faith as well and I was better able to resist those temptations to go back. After I had lived with them for a year, Mike and Jenny came to me and told me they thought I was ready to take my first steps on my own again.

Even though I was in my forties, I was scared to go out on my own. It felt a little like the first time I had left home, twenty years earlier. Everything was new and unknown to me. I didn't know exactly what to expect or what would happen, but I did know that I had a strong, sure friend in Jesus Christ.

I was able to find a Christian roommate and move in with her and I also felt like God was calling me to a new church home as well. I had learned and grown a lot at Maple Grove Assembly of God, but I didn't feel I fit in there anymore. I had heard about a church called Speak the Word that was nearby and I could feel my heart being called there.

I met with Jenny, Mike, and Pastor Gary to tell them what God was laying on my heart. I didn't want to just leave the church without anyone knowing where I went. They all encouraged me to set up an appointment with the heads of the singles ministry at Speak the Word and tell them my story. I did and I was welcomed and they agreed to help keep me accountable.

I didn't leave Maple Grove Assembly of God immediately. Instead, I started going to the singles night on Friday nights at Speak the Word. After about a month, I also started attending the Wednesday night services. I didn't speak to anyone for quite a while; I just sat in the service and absorbed the environment. Finally, after several months of going to the service on Wednesday nights, I stepped out and began introducing myself to some of the other people who attended.

I met one of the pastors of Speak the Word while I was working out at Lifetime Fitness. I was watching some young men play basketball when a woman walked up to watch them as well. I recognized her as Pastor Rachael Morickson and so I introduced myself. Her son was one of the boys playing basketball on the court. While we watched the boys play, I told her that I had come out of the lesbian lifestyle and that I was attending her church. She welcomed me and then, after talking with me a little more, asked me to help her son out with his basketball skills. I began working out with her son Tyrone and developed a friendship with Pastor Rachael as well.

I was still attending both Maple Grove Assembly of God and Speak the Word, but I finally decided that it was time for me to move to Speak the Word full time. I made an appointment with Pastor Gary, he gave me his blessing, and I began attending Speak the Word on Sundays as well as on Wednesdays and Fridays—just like those little girls I had wondered about all those years before.

Every time I went to church, I met someone new. I greeted every new person I met with the same introduction. "Hi, I'm Janet. I just came out of the lesbian lifestyle." Even though I must have shocked a few people, I wanted everyone to know where I was coming from right away. If they were going to reject me for my past, I wanted them to do it immediately so I wouldn't get hurt. My blunt greeting went on for quite a while until Pastor Ryan, another pastor at Speak the Word, finally talked to me. He told me I didn't have to wear a sign of guilt around my neck anymore; that I had been forgiven by the blood of Christ. I followed Pastor Ryan's advice, although I still shared my testimony with those I met. I just didn't tell them that I used to be a lesbian right after saying hello.

I started seeking out the advice of Pastor Rachael as well. I had been dressing like a man for so many years that I no longer knew what it meant to look and dress in a feminine manner. Pastor Rachael took me shopping for clothes and another woman from church began teaching me how to walk like a woman and how to put on makeup.

In the years since those early first steps of faith, I have gradually gained confidence as a woman. I know that I have made a fool of myself trying to learn how to walk in heels and there are definitely days when I feel more comfortable in a sweatshirt and blue jeans, but I have been learning little by little. I have grown my hair out and regularly get my nails done. God even blessed me with an opportunity to meet the President of the United States at a fundraiser in 2006. President Bush told me I was a beautiful person—what a far cry from my days of short hair and men's clothes!

More than any outward attire, however, I have been learning how to be satisfied with myself and how to run into the arms of my heavenly Father. I know I can run to Him with any problem, any defeat, any joy, and any victory and that His perfect and unfailing love will always be there to comfort me.

I still have thoughts about the homosexual lifestyle from time to time, but I no longer have any desire to return to it. My thoughts and desires have changed since I returned to a relationship with Jesus Christ. My hope for my personal life is now to one day have a husband, and my desire, instead of returning to the homosexual lifestyle, is to help those who are struggling with the same things that I struggled with for so long.

God has been opening up many doors for me to share my story and I believe there will be many more opportunities. He has allowed me to share in churches, colleges, on the radio, and on Christian television. Even though my road has been long and hard, from this point forward, my message will always be the same: my freedom has been found only in the love of Jesus Christ and I know that what God has done for me, He can also do for you.

PART II:
THE MESSAGE

Chapter 7

FOR THOSE WHO STRUGGLE

WHEN GOD CALLS, HE CALLS IN LOVE, BUT SOMEtimes the pain in life can be so bad that love seems only a far-off dream. Sometimes the hurt in our hearts cuts so deeply that even hope seems impossible. I am writing this because I have been at that place in my life, where I felt I was without love and without hope, and I want my story to be an example for all who feel that they are in a similar place. I know that love can be found and hope can be renewed, but only if we turn to the One who truly loves us.

In this chapter, I would like to speak directly to those who may be reading this book while living or perhaps exploring a homosexual lifestyle and I want to tell you that God loves you.

God.
Loves.
You.

And He loves *you*—there are no ifs, ands, or buts. He loves you no matter who you are, no matter what you've done, no matter where you've been. Nothing will ever, *ever* change His love for you. God loves you with a fierce passion; He loves you with a gentle grace. He sees every tear you shed and He cries with you. He feels every hurt you endure as if the pain were His own. God cries out to each and every one of us, desperately, longingly, begging us to let Him wash away our pain. He is calling you; calling you to come and rest in His arms, away from the tears, away from the hurt.

I've been hurt. I know what it's like to experience the roughness of life, getting up only to get knocked down again. You know from my story that I lived in an abusive home, with a stern mother and her drunken boyfriend. I was sexually abused twice. My real father abandoned me. Everyone told me I looked like a boy. I was never able to get attention from my mother unless I did something wrong. That is the "love" I grew up with and that love hurt. *A lot!*

I know what it's like to cry myself to sleep, crying because there is no one to talk with, no one to encourage me, no one who understands my heart. Every time something else happened in my young life, another wound opened up on the inside. And every one of those wounds changed me.

I wanted to escape the nightmare I had been born into and so I grew harder than a little girl should ever become. I became angry and began fighting back. I didn't want anyone ever to hurt me again, so I tried to hurt everyone else before they could hurt me. I became a bully and a fighter, at school and with my brothers and sisters.

I felt so empty inside. Nothing I tried was able to fill the void in my heart that was driving my desperate search. I wanted to make something of myself, finding a way to somehow make people love me. The type of love I had experienced in my life wasn't enough and I knew it. I needed something more.

I tried seeking love through relationships and began experimenting with boys, but I found out that most of my boyfriends just wanted me for sex. My feelings for men were already distorted because of the abuse and neglect in my childhood. I knew that I didn't want to be just a sexual object, so I decided that a heterosexual relationship wasn't enough for me and I began seeking women.

I tried to fill the emptiness inside of me by having relationships with women for fourteen years. During that time, I jumped from relationship to relationship, desperately hoping that the next relationship would be the last, that I would finally find what I was looking for to fill my aching heart.

The relationships weren't enough. I kept trying to mix in smoking or drugs to help meet my needs, but they only tore my life further apart. Nothing helped and I hurt more than ever.

Finally—*finally*—I turned to God.

God had been standing by my side my entire life, every moment seeing my hurt and pain, longing to heal me, and calling me back to Him all along. He was calling when we moved in with my grandmother, right next door to a church. He was calling when I followed Cindy to Minnesota and she helped me enroll in a Bible school. He was calling when I began going to church in Minneapolis and when I lived at Parkhouse. My life was a living example of Revelation 3:20, in which Christ says, "Behold, I stand at the door and knock: if any man hears my voice and opens the door, I will come in and eat with him and he with me."

As I look back, I can see God's hand in my life again and again: when I began talking about God for no apparent reason while sitting in gay bars, when I met Lucy and John at Bethlehem Baptist, when I kept driving past Maple Grove Assembly of God, somehow knowing that I would one day attend there, and when I met a woman from that very church I passed by every day. God kept calling me. He loved me. And He never gave up.

My life didn't magically get better when I finally began to listen to God's call on my life. I began to understand that God really, truly loved me, but that love also called my attention to the way I had been living. I knew there were things in my life that I had ignored for too long and I needed to make them right.

Little by little, with the help of God and with the prayer and support of my friends, I began to leave my old lifestyle behind. It was far from easy. My life was a constant struggle that, on the bad days, became a war. I still hurt from all the wounds that had been inflicted throughout my life and I still had my problems, but when I turned to God, I knew that I could bring all my troubles to Him. He became my strength. He began filling the emptiness in my heart, binding up the hurts and healing them. For the first time in my life, I began to feel at peace.

Perhaps your story is similar to mine. You may have been abused, deeply hurt, neglected, abandoned, or ridiculed at different times in your life. You may feel as if you have been singled out as being different, a feeling that hurts even after you try to embrace it. Even if your story is one of love and acceptance, I believe that we still have something in common: we are all searching for something to fill the emptiness inside.

Life itself is a struggle and a search for identity, no matter whether you are heterosexual or homosexual, but for those of us who have considered or pursued homosexuality, the search becomes even more difficult. We don't seem to fit in with the rest of the world. Somehow, things just never seem to work out right. No one seems to understand what it is like to struggle so much about who you are. Our confusion and our loneliness cause us to begin searching, looking for ways to define who we are, looking for someone that even comes close to understanding. And nothing, no one, ever seems to satisfy.

If my words are touching your heart in any way, please, let my life be a living testimony. I speak from experience: only God's love can truly satisfy; only He can give meaning and identity; and God's love can only be found in Jesus Christ.

Jesus said this in Matthew 11:28–30, "Come to me, all you who are weary and burdened, and I will give you rest. Take my yoke upon you and learn from me, for I am gentle and humble in heart, and you will find rest for your souls. For my yoke is easy and my burden is light."

But what does it mean to come to Jesus Christ? How would following Him impact and change your life?

I am sure you have probably heard more times than you can count that the Bible condemns homosexuality and that homosexuality is a sin. It is a message the church and most Christians have done a very good job spreading. Where they have failed is in reaching out to those they condemn. Where they have failed is in watching for sin in their own lives. Where they have failed is in telling those in the homosexual community that God loves them.

I will not mince words or make excuses. The Bible says that homosexual behavior is a sin. It is *not* to be practiced. Leviticus 18:22 and 20:13 both call homosexuality detestable, Romans 1:26–27 calls it unnatural, and 1 Corinthians 6:9–10 says that homosexual offenders will not inherit the kingdom of God.

The Bible leaves no wiggle room on the issue of homosexuality. The commands against homosexuality cannot be explained away by saying that they were for a different time and a different culture just because Leviticus was written some fifteen hundred years before Romans and 1 Corinthians, or because the cultures of the nomadic Hebrews escaping Egypt and the Roman Empire were vastly different from each other. God's law remains the same through the ages and among all the cultures and we have no reason to think we are any different. Homosexual behavior is still as much a sin today as it was two thousand years ago.

Having said that homosexuality is a sin, I do not believe that it is a special sin. From an eternal perspective, homosexuality is no different than adultery, coveting, lying, doing drugs, premarital sex, or placing anything in our lives before God. Each sin has different consequences; homosexuality is certainly different than stealing, but *all* sins are the same in that they separate mankind from God.

God loves each and every one of us and cannot bear to have us separated from His presence. Love is the reason Jesus went willingly to the cross to die, to cover our sins with His perfection. He became the perfect sacrifice when no other sacrifice would do and He took away our sins so we may spend eternity in His presence. He offers eternal life as a gift, free of charge; love there for the taking. He desperately wants to begin a relationship with us, but He will not force us.

If you truly begin a relationship with Jesus Christ, I believe His love will transform your life as it has transformed mine. You will find a peace that far surpasses anything you have ever known. Your goals, your dreams, and your desires will gradually begin to change and align themselves with God's plan for your life. You will start seeing more and more of that plan as you follow God and obey His Word.

What is that plan? It can be both terrifying and humbling to think that God has a plan for the life of every person. "How does God know what is good for me?" you may ask. "What if He has a plan I will hate?" God will never make you act against your will; you have a choice whether or not you will follow Him. God loves you so much and knows you so intimately, as the Bible tells us in Matthew 10:30, that even the very hairs on our heads are all numbered. God knows your secret hopes and your deepest desires. He knows because He created you.

In Jeremiah 29:11–14, God spoke specifically to the nation of Israel, but what He said was for everyone, "For I know the plans I have for you...plans to prosper you and not to harm you, plans to give you a hope and a future. Then you will call upon me and come and pray to me and I will listen to you. You will seek me and find me when you seek me with all your heart. I will be found by you...and will bring you back from captivity."

The captivity God was talking about was, in part, sin. Sin takes away freedom because it calls you back to it again and again. Sin becomes an addiction we cannot escape by ourselves. Consider my life with drugs: I had a genuine need for love, which is certainly not wrong, but I tried to fill that need with the wrong thing. Soon I became hooked on drugs. They called me back so many times that I became addicted. Sin is the same way. It penetrates into every area of our lives, becoming a physical, emotional, mental, and spiritual addiction. Sin will take you further than you want to go and it will keep you longer than you want to stay. God's love is our only freedom from sin, and that love is only found through a relationship with Jesus Christ.

God's love isn't just a one-time event. It never stops. Because of His unending love, God doesn't want those who have begun a relationship with Him to fall back into sin. He gave us the Bible, complete with all of its guidelines for life, because He loves us and He wants what is best for us.

The laws written down in the Bible were written to keep us from being hurt by sin. Just as a father or mother will tell their child to eat his or her vegetables or not to cross a busy street alone or not to touch a hot stove, so God, our heavenly Father, has given us instructions about what we should and shouldn't do. A child may not understand that if he crosses a street, a car may hit him, or if he touches a hot stove, he will get burned. The child may not know, but his parents do, and if they see him about to run across the street or reaching out for the stove, they will stop him and discipline him so he won't do it again. A little tough love on the part of the parents is far better than the consequences of disobedience on the part of the child: being killed by a car or burned by the stove. So it is with God, even when we don't always understand the reasoning behind His commands. He gave us laws to protect us because He loves each and every one of us as a precious son or daughter.

It isn't easy to completely obey God all the time or even some of the time. I try and fail every day. I fall and give into temptations every day. I sin every day. I'm far from perfect, but now that I've begun a personal relationship with Jesus Christ, I know that when I sin, I can ask for forgiveness and I will be forgiven. Colossians 1:13–14 says, "For he has rescued us from the dominion of darkness and brought us into the kingdom of the Son he loves, in whom we have redemption, the forgiveness of sins." I know that when I face temptation, I can ask for strength and it will be given to me. First Corinthians 10:13 says, "No temptation has seized you except what is common to man. And God is faithful; he will not let you be tempted beyond what you can bear. But when you are tempted, he will also provide a way out so that you can stand up under it."

When I finally turned my life over to God, His love shed light on the things I needed to change. He began calling me out of homosexuality and I followed His call in obedience. It wasn't easy. It wasn't quick. There were certainly many times I tried to go back, but God's love provided a way out for me, first through a Bible study of caring women and then through a loving family. I believe with all my heart that God's love can do the same for you.

My search for love took me many places and I learned many things. I now know drugs and smoking will never fulfill me or provide answers. I will never find peace from a relationship with a woman, but neither will I find peace from a relationship with a man. Only Jesus Christ has given me peace. Only Jesus Christ has given me hope. Only Jesus Christ has given me the love I now know I had been seeking my entire life.

I'm not trying to change you into a heterosexual. I know that when I was living a homosexual lifestyle, if someone had tried to make me become a heterosexual, I would have resisted with every last ounce of my strength. No one can force anyone to be someone they don't want to be.

Rather than trying to change you, my message is simply this: God loves you.

God loves you and He is calling you. He wants to welcome you with open arms. He wants to heal your hurts. He wants to begin a relationship with you, wiping away your tears and washing away your sins. He has a plan for your life.

My life is proof that God can set a person free from addiction, captivity, fear, and loneliness. You can be set free from homosexuality; you don't have to live and struggle with it for your entire life. Seek God and you will find Him.

I don't believe you need to change everything in your life before you begin a personal relationship with Jesus Christ. You don't have to make yourself perfect to call out God's name, to bury your head in His shoulder and cry the tears you've been holding back for so long. God doesn't work that way. He wants you to come to Him just as you are and He will help you fix your problems, rather than forcing you to fix them before He accepts you. All you need to do is call out to Him, ask for forgiveness and repent of your sins. If you truly choose to follow Him, your life will begin to change. God's love will transform you. He will provide a way out. He will fill you with hope, surround you with His gentle peace, and comfort you with His unending love.

Chapter 8

FOR THE CHURCH

W HEN GOD CALLS, HE CALLS IN LOVE, AND IT IS A message that needs to be communicated through those who follow Him, through those who call themselves Christians, through the church. God's message of love must be spoken in love.

In this chapter, I would like to speak to the church, to those who claim to follow Christ. Hope and love have been given to us. We have the Word of God to guide our steps. We have the life and words of the Son of God as an example for us to live our lives. Eternal salvation has been placed as a crown on our heads. The very Creator of heaven and earth has chosen to call us His children. We have been given all of these things and all that has been commanded to us is that we must love.

We *must* love.

We must love because love is the only force that can break down walls and mend broken hearts. Love is a beacon shining into the dark for all those lost in the sea of life, about to crash on the shores of eternity. Love is a helping hand to the hurting, to those who have nothing left. We must love because our love defines us.

Jesus said in John 13:35, "By this all men will know that you are my disciples, if you love one another." The apostle Paul also talked about love in 1 Corinthians 13:1–3, saying,

"If I speak in the tongues of men and of angels, but have not love, I am only a resounding gong or clanging cymbal. If I have the gift of prophecy and can fathom all mysteries and all knowledge, and if I have a faith that can move mountains, but have not love, I am nothing. If I give all I possess to the poor and surrender my body to the flames, but have not love, I gain nothing."

In our busy and modern world, we have wandered away from this vital message of love. We speak of love day after day, in sentence after sentence, yet it is not the love of God that is present in our lives. Our love has somehow transformed itself into something entirely different, something that craves self-satisfaction.

My dear brothers and sisters in Christ, please hear me. As the church, the body of Christ, we have failed to love as we should. Our love must start with our relationship with God. For some, however, their love for Christ has faded into duty—a chore to which they must attend before turning back to having fun. Too often our relationship with the Creator becomes one of convenience; a friendship that is looked to only if it fits into our schedules. God often is viewed as a last resort, a Friend we turn to only when we find ourselves in the worst kinds of trouble. Church, this cannot be.

The time we spend deepening our relationship with Jesus Christ directly affects every area of our lives because God's love has the power to transform lives. It changes the core of every individual who receives it. Jesus said in Matthew 12:34 that "out of the overflow of the heart the mouth speaks." If our hearts are full of God's love as a result of having taken the time to pursue a relationship with Him, then our actions, our words, and our lives will follow suit.

What good will come of more money from the tithes and offerings in our churches if the poor down the street are still hungry and homeless? How does attending church once, twice, or three times a week demonstrate God's love when we leave our neighbors sick and alone? What lessons will be learned by our children if we give them new toys and games and yet neglect to spend time with them, teaching them what is right and true? How holy are we if we publicly denounce sin in others and yet fail to address it in our own lives?

Brothers and sisters, we must love, and that love must start in our relationship with Jesus Christ. The church is slipping fast and it is because we have lost sight of our Lord and Savior. All around, Christians are becoming more like the world we call so evil, even as we claim to be different and set apart in holiness. Jesus has these words to say to us, found in Matthew 7:3–5, "Why do you look at the speck of sawdust in your brother's eye and pay no attention to the plank in your own eye? How can you say to your brother, 'Let me take the speck out of your eye,' when all the time there is a plank in your own eye? You hypocrite, first take the plank out of your own eye, and then you will see clearly to remove the speck from your brother's eye."

The plank in the eye of today's church is that we have wandered away from our foundation, Jesus Christ. We have forgotten His example of love and we have forgotten His example of righteousness. We don't bother to obey Scripture or to even see what it says. God is calling us back to Him, calling us to pure hearts, righteous lives, and loving actions.

We *desperately* need to rediscover our first love and the faith that so brightly lit our hearts when we first came to Christ. It can only be done if we seek God with all of our hearts. It can only be done if we make a commitment to pursue a relationship with God daily, spending time in prayer and in Scripture.

I have struggled in my relationship with Christ as much as anyone. Even during the writing of this book, I've had my highs and lows, I've had days or even weeks go by without reading Scripture, and I've had times when I've felt like giving up. It isn't easy. Being a Christian isn't easy, but God's love is too important to give up, to follow the empty desires and promises of the world. We must struggle on and we must persevere.

I have been emphasizing our personal and daily relationship with Christ because we cannot help or love those around us without first being filled with love ourselves. Many churches have been focusing on building a new facility or on gaining a larger congregation instead of actually ministering to the hurting world around them. Many individuals do the same by seeking worldly wealth and possessions instead of heavenly treasures, stored up by loving others and obeying God's Word.

Our loss of focus on Christ has caused the church to be caught by surprise in a number of ways as we suddenly find our beliefs and our actions becoming more like the rest of the world. Although there are many areas that we have failed to guard against, one such area that has crept up on us is the growing issue of homosexuality.

As homosexuality has become more common, Christians have struggled with how they should respond. Some have taken to the streets in protest. Others have openly embraced homosexuality, allowing gays and lesbians into the pulpit and leadership positions in their churches. And, overwhelmingly, most Christians are simply trying to ignore homosexuality, hoping they can wait out the issue until it goes away because they don't want to deal with conflict or sin.

Dear church, we can be apathetic no longer. We cannot ignore homosexuality. The homosexual community is small, but it isn't going away. Instead, it has become a vocal and influential part of our society. The church has been responding to homosexuals and homosexuality with mixed signals, but now we must speak with one voice, and we must act. We must speak and act with God's love.

But how?

The Bible clearly states that homosexuality is a sin. Those who try to explain away the scriptures dealing with homosexuality as being culturally and morally outdated are growing in number, but they are wrong. Parts of the Bible cannot be ignored or taken out simply because they tell us things we don't want to hear. When I was living in homosexuality, I knew I was sinning. The Bible told me, my conscience told me, and many people in my life told me. Unfortunately, I also had many people telling me that what I was doing was simply a lifestyle choice and not a sin; people including the priest Haley and I went to for counseling.

As Christians, we cannot make excuses for sin—any sin.

We *must* make a stand for righteousness and purity. It *must* begin in our own lives and be demonstrated by the church as a whole, by everyone from pulpit to pew. We *must* set an example by the way we live our lives or we will have no moral authority to lead others. There *must* be a concentrated effort to renew the family life by preaching and practicing abstinence until marriage, marriage for life, and stronger parental involvement in the lives of their children.

Homosexuality is not the only sin. However, far too many Christians view it as such because we want to draw attention away from the sin in our own lives. We have singled out homosexuality and treated those struggling with a homosexual inclination as if they were worse than rapists, adulterers, those who engage in premarital sex, those who look at pornography, or even those who have problems with lust. While every sin may have different consequences during our life on earth, all sins are alike in that they separate us from God. Romans 3:23 tells us, "All have sinned."

Church, we need to end our hypocrisy. Though homosexuality is a sin, those who struggle with it are not the enemy. Ephesians 6:12 says, "For our struggle is not against flesh and blood, but against the rulers, against the authorities, against the powers of this dark world and against the spiritual forces of evil in the heavenly realms." Instead of condemning, let us offer a helping hand to those who struggle with homosexuality, or any other sin, and let us encourage one another toward righteousness.

For those in the church who hold up signs painted with slogans like, "God hates gays," I ask you to carefully consider the message you are sending. "God hates gays" isn't true. God doesn't hate anyone. In fact, this is what 1 John 4:20–21 says, "If anyone says, 'I love God,' yet hates his brother, he is a liar. For anyone who does not love his brother, whom he has seen, cannot love God, whom he has not seen. And he has given us this command: Whoever loves God must also love his brother."

God is love. He loved us so much that He sent His only Son to die for a sinful world, a world that all of us are a part of and in which all of us have participated. With such an example set before us, if we claim to be followers of Christ Jesus, our message *cannot* be hate. It *must* be love, especially if we hope to make an eternal difference in the lives of those around us.

During the course of Jesus' ministry on earth, He frequently ministered to those who were hurting, sick, poor, or hungry. He ministered to the souls of the people, but He also did not neglect their physical needs. Jesus' spiritual and moral authority were based on His righteous life, but people came to Him for His ability to meet their physical needs as well. Dearest church, we need to follow Christ's example.

But what are the specific needs of the homosexual community? How can the church meet the desires of those struggling with homosexuality and help them heal the hurts laid into their hearts? How can we make an eternal difference in their lives?

My own experience as a former lesbian leads me to believe that many in the homosexual community are searching for love and acceptance. I know my own search was driven by the events and abuse in my childhood, by never being able to fit into society's cookie-cutter image of what a young girl or woman should be like. I desperately needed to find love, to feel loved, and to experience love.

Church, let us open our arms to the hurting. Let us lead the way. Let us take the first step. It starts with how we treat others. Do not look down on others because they have sinned. We *all* have sinned. We can and should call sin what it is, but our place is not to judge; our place is to love and to support each other as we all try to become more Christ-like. Let us lift up those who are struggling and encourage them in love to stop sinning and turn toward a relationship with Jesus Christ.

We need to do more, however, than merely treating those struggling with homosexuality nicely. I would like to suggest something that some might consider a radical way of reaching out to the homosexual community, but it is an option I believe could bear incredible fruit: let us open the doors of our churches and homes to those who wish to leave homosexuality.

Very few churches offer any sort of ministry to those who struggle with homosexual feelings or behavior. The church as a whole hasn't taken the time to educate itself about homosexuality or about how to minister to those caught in that lifestyle. We will never be able to make a difference in the lives of gays and lesbians unless we are able to offer a realistic alternative, a way out. It starts by opening our doors.

I do not wish to suggest that we should go out and force gays and lesbians to become straight. That is the last thing we should do. Rather, we should open our doors and invite them in to experience the real love that a relationship with Jesus Christ offers. If they accept Jesus as their personal Lord and Savior, we then need to be able to help them realize they can be set free from homosexuality, though leaving homosexuality must always be a choice that the individual makes and never one that is made for them.

When I first began attending Maple Grove Assembly of God, I quickly became involved in a women's Bible study. For the first time in years, I worked with women in a non-sexual manner and they were able to teach me so much. I learned about my identity as a woman, how to dress like a woman, how to walk like a woman, even how to put on make-up. God is not consumed with the outer appearance, however, but looks first at the heart. Most importantly, I learned through those women about the love of God and how He was calling me to live a righteous life.

The Bible study I attended wasn't specifically designed for people to come out of homosexuality, but it didn't matter. Those women loved me like a sister and a daughter. They prayed for me—*they accepted me for who I was.* All the while they encouraged me to become more, and to be all the Lord made me to be. They gave me advice and instruction, but they also helped meet my physical needs. For their actions, instruction, and love, I am eternally grateful.

I want to challenge you as a reader: does your church have any ministries that reach out to those who struggle with homosexuality? If a gay or lesbian were to walk into your church on Sunday, how would they be treated? Would you be able to walk up to them and greet them with a smile? Would you be able to tell them that God loves them, no matter what they've done, no matter where they've been?

Nothing demonstrated love to me more than when one of the women from my Bible study invited me to live with her and her family. She opened her heart and her home to me and, in so doing, made a great difference in my life. There was nothing sexual about her invitation; instead, I was able to see how a healthy family functioned, an example I had never had.

I saw how men were supposed to love their wives, how women were supposed to love their husbands, and how parents were supposed to love their children. It wasn't a perfect family, of course. I saw their fights and their defeats, but I also saw how they made up and how they prayed together and read Scripture through the bad times and the good. It was completely different from the horrors of my own childhood.

Piece by piece, I saw the shattered fragments of my self-image, my sexuality, and my spirituality restored and healed. Even though it lasted only a year, staying with a Christian family was a second childhood for me. It didn't erase all my bad memories, but it showed me how things were supposed to be. During that year, I was able to experience real family love and it made a difference in my life.

Brothers and sisters, I am not suggesting that every family in the church should open their homes to people coming out of the homosexual lifestyle. It is a difficult thing to accept anyone to live in your house for an extended period of time and, quite frankly, many families in our churches aren't strong enough to do so. However, I believe if more families would open their homes to host, mentor, and love those who want to come out of homosexuality, there would be an enormous ministry opportunity with the homosexual community.

The message of love I received from my time with a family gave me a sense of belonging and a purpose. At times it was a tough love because I was removed from my old lifestyle, but it was also a healing love. Church, let us model ourselves after the love described in 1 Corinthians 13:4–7 which says, "Love is patient, love is kind. It does not envy, it does not boast, it is not proud. It is not rude, it is not self-seeking, it is not easily angered, it keeps no record of wrongs. Love does not delight in evil but rejoices with the truth. It always protects, always trusts, always hopes, always perseveres."

If we open our churches and homes in love, think of the message that would be sent to those struggling with homosexuality. Instead of, "God hates fags," it would be, "God loves you—and we love you, too." While I don't believe the entire homosexual community would come racing to the church doors, I do believe that, quietly but steadily, a strong and open message of love would break down the walls and barriers that have been built up between gays and lesbians and the church.

I believe we would see the miracle of changed lives again and again, in the church and in the homosexual community.

We need to send out a consistent message, one that speaks and acts in love while not compromising values or becoming accepting of sin. This is a message that needs to reach not only the homosexual community, but also our churches. For any family or any church that hopes or desires to open its doors in ministry, let it first make sure the lives of its members are being lived according to the righteous example Jesus set before us. As the body of Christ, we need to repent of our own sins and turn back to God and then we will be able to minister and counsel others. Jesus warns us in Revelation 3:2–3, "Wake up! Strengthen what remains and is about to die, for I have not found your deeds complete in the sight of my God. Remember, therefore, what you have received and heard; obey it, and repent. But if you do not wake up, I will come like a thief, and you will not know at what time I will come to you."

Chapter 9

FOR PARENTS

Whenever God calls, He calls in love. In a perfect world, God's love should first be felt through the love of our families, however, such is not always the case. I know that the type of love I felt in my earlier years wasn't at all like the love of God. I experienced a harsh, biting love that confused me and changed me.

In this chapter, I would like to address the role family life and parental love have in affecting and even creating homosexuality in children. It is a larger role than many may think, and in today's society it is a role that is often overlooked and ignored.

In my own life, my family situation created a difficult environment in which to grow up. To put it bluntly, my home life was a broken mess.

I eventually made a choice to enter a homosexual relationship and I will not place the responsibility of that choice on anything or anyone but myself. Though I don't believe that my childhood *caused* my homosexuality, I believe the difficulty of my childhood years was a very large contributing factor to my willingness to experiment with homosexuality.

Because I lacked a stable and nurturing home environment, I sought escape. As I mentioned before, my escape often took the form of experimentation. Children react in different ways when confronted with situations outside of their control. I don't think it was any coincidence that my brother Robert also turned to homosexuality because he grew up in the same environment I did. While I don't know if he was ever sexually abused, he did receive the same physical abuse I did and he also lacked a father figure in his life. Instead of becoming hard inside, however, I believe Robert went in the opposite direction. I turned all of my hurt outward and made it a hard shell, but he turned it inward where no one could see it.

There are many families like mine. Divorce rates are far too high and single-parent families are much too common. Alcoholism, physical abuse, and sexual abuse are often present in the homes of many of today's families. Parents are absent, neglectful, and abusive while children are lost, disobedient, disrespectful, and forced to grow up all too quickly.

Today's family is in a tailspin and the problem begins with our willingness to divorce, even before thoughts of marriage have entered our minds. We live in a disposable society in which, if something doesn't work, we throw it away and try to find something better. Disposability doesn't work with marriage. Marriage is meant to be a lifelong commitment or nothing at all.

Many marriages are also hurting and end in divorce because we seek out relationships of convenience, or more specifically, physical convenience. Too many couples engage in extra-marital sexual activity and it is killing marriage relationships.

The Bible clearly warns against premarital sex, or fornication (see 1 Corinthians 6:9; Galatians 5:19), and it does so for good reason, naming it as a sin. The act of sex creates an intimate bond between two people, which is vital within a marriage, but premarital sex can create that bond before any other foundation is laid. It is absolutely necessary to have emotional, spiritual, and mental connections laid down as a proper foundation for a relationship to be successful; the physical cannot stand alone. One of the reasons premarital sexual activity is so dangerous is that it creates a false sense of familiarity that can cover over the other areas that are also needed to make a relationship and marriage work. As a result, many couples who get married after having premarital sex find that they don't know each other as well as they should, which gives them a rocky road to travel from the start.

Another side effect of widespread premarital sexual activity has been a rise in the number of children born outside marriage. This, combined with divorce, has created a growing number of single-parent families and the effect on children has been devastating.

What does the family have to do with homosexuality? It has *everything* to do with it. Our families are where we receive the first messages that shape our identity. Those first messages are critically important because they create lasting impressions on our personalities for either good or bad.

Our parents are the ones who first teach us how to relate to the world around us, including how to treat and interact with those of the opposite sex. We learn about this relationship by watching our parents' example. Parents, this is an incredible responsibility, and it begins the moment you bring a child into the world.

Men, what lessons do you teach your children if you constantly yell at your wife, get into fights with her, or even abuse her? Women, what lessons do you teach your children if you always complain about your husband or if you have arguments all the time? What message do you send if you ignore your spouse, never laughing with or enjoying each other? Children see and they learn and imitate. It is because of this mimicry that destructive and abusive behavior often is passed from one generation to the next.

In my life, I believe one of my most significant needs was to have a strong father figure. I didn't have a father to hold me in his arms at night and read me stories. I didn't have a father to run to and hug every night when he came home from work. I didn't have a father who would carefully investigate and question potential boyfriends or prom dates or come to any of my sporting events. I had no one to run to, no one to protect me. The men in my life were either absent or abusive.

Sadly, in this area of father hunger my story is not unique. The media has tried to downplay the importance of marriage and fatherhood, but the consequences are tearing our families and children apart. Throughout society, men are not being men. The responsibilities that come with being in a marriage relationship and fathering children need to be realized and men need to start stepping up to fill those roles.

There is absolutely no substitute for a father. I cannot begin to think of how my life would have been different if my father or even one of my stepfathers had taken an active and healthy interest in my life. My mother tried her best in the only way she knew how, and perhaps her sternness was partially to make up for our lack of a male role model, but there was no way she could ever be both a mother and a father to me and my siblings.

Husbands and fathers, you need to realize that you have a very vital role in the lives of your wives and your children. For marriage, realize that you need to love and cherish your wife, as if she were part of your own body, as Paul teaches in Ephesians 5. She is your partner in a relationship that should last your entire lives; treat her as such.

Concerning children, Scripture offers this advice in Proverbs 22:6, "Train a child in the way he should go, and when he is old he will not turn from it." Consider how you train and raise your children. No matter what you teach or how you instruct, the most influential tool you have is the way you lead your own life. Your example will continue to influence your children for the rest of their lives, for good or bad. Even our view of God is closely related to how we view our fathers. Fathers, how are you shaping the lives of your children by your example?

Finally, men need to be leaders. Our families, our churches, and our society have all suffered because men have been withdrawing from responsibility and leadership. Despite the attention given to women's rights in recent years, much of which I believe was necessary, someone still needs to be the leader. Scripture teaches us very clearly that the leadership roles should be given to men.

Leadership is nothing unless it is first a spiritual leadership. Husbands, fathers, do you pray for your wives and your children? Do you encourage them in their relationships with God? Do you read Scripture and teach them in your home? Most importantly, what kind of spiritual example do you lead with your own life?

Wives and mothers, you have no less a responsibility. Many of the same responsibilities given to men also hold true for women. A wife must love and respect her husband and she should also live her life according to the principles set forth in Scripture.

The Bible teaches in Ephesians 5 that the man should be the head of the household and that the woman should be in submission to him, but this is a Scripture that is often blown out of proportion and blatantly misinterpreted by both Christians and non-Christians alike. Ephesians 5:15–24 says:

> Be very careful, then, how you live—not as unwise but as wise, making the most of every opportunity, because the days are evil. Therefore do not be foolish, but understand what the Lord's will is. Do not get drunk on wine, which leads to debauchery. Instead, be filled with the Spirit. Speak to one another with psalms, hymns, and spiritual songs. Sing and make music in your heart to the Lord, always giving thanks to God the Father for everything, in the name of our Lord Jesus Christ. Submit to one another out of reverence for Christ. Wives, submit to your husbands as to the Lord. For the husband is the head of the wife as Christ is the head of the church, his body, of which he is the Savior. Now as the church submits to Christ, so also wives should submit to their husbands in everything.

Many have taken this passage to mean that women should be almost enslaved to the wills of their husbands, unable to do or say anything without his consent. This is simply not true and it is not what the Bible is saying. Consider the verse above, which says that all believers should "submit to each other out of reverence for Christ." In many ways, wives should submit to their husbands in the same way any believer should submit to other believers, specifically by living according to the lifestyle the apostle Paul lays out earlier in the chapter. This mutual submission is an accountability to be held to God's standards, an accountability in which *both* husband and wife are called to participate.

Paul does, however, establish the husband as the head of the marriage relationship and the submission that he talks about is deference. While the husband and wife are a team and need to hold each other accountable to live according to God's standards, the husband does receive the leadership mantle in the relationship. As the leader, he should make the final decision in matters concerning the family according to Godly principles, though this does *not* mean he can or should make decisions without first discussing them with his wife.

Wives, how then should you act? Proverbs 31 speaks extensively about a wife of noble character who is hardworking and praised by both her husband and her children. Verse 30 tells us her secret, "Charm is deceptive, and beauty is fleeting; but a woman who fears the Lord is to be praised."

Women, though your husbands are to be the spiritual heads of your households, your spiritual responsibilities are not small either. Encourage your husbands in the Lord, challenge them, and remind them to read Scripture and to pray. The power of a praying wife should not be underestimated. There will be times when your husband will stumble or be discouraged, and it is then that you will need to step in and stand by him in word, deed, and prayer. Help give him the courage to become the man of God he needs to become.

Mothers, you generally will have a greater opportunity to influence your children in the first years of their lives than will your husbands because the mother naturally develops a bond earlier than the father. Begin teaching your children spiritual habits and morals from an early age, and when they grow older, they won't leave them behind. Remember, your own personal example will speak loudest to them.

I realize there are many single parent and broken homes and not everyone has the opportunity to return to or enter into a healthy marriage relationship. There are many struggles and difficulties those parents will face that a husband and wife together will not. You may not be able to change the past, but there can still be healing, both for your children and for yourself. Seek out Jesus and you will find Him; call out and He will answer. He can more than make up for the love that has been lost and He can heal the pain that has been suffered.

There can be a lot of pain growing up. I lived through so much of it and I know there are children everywhere who experience many of the same things I did. Adolescence is hard enough, but when you add abuse, alcoholic parents, divorce, poverty, severe ridicule at school, a single-parent home, and countless other factors, both childhood and adolescence can become nightmares.

There are many questions surrounding the identification and prevention of homosexuality in children and the answers will vary and, at times, even conflict. I am not a child psychologist, but I do have some practical advice for any parent, whether their children exhibit seemingly homosexual tendencies or not: spend time with your children, find out who they really are, and know who their friends are.

Our society has structured itself in such a way that everyone is busy all the time and each generation seems to get progressively busier. We are busy with work, with social functions, with sporting events, and with eating out; we are always doing something and always going somewhere. Unfortunately, our relationships, especially our relationships with our spouses and children, often suffer because of the busyness with which we surround ourselves.

Our children are just as busy as any adult. Since I was called out of the homosexual lifestyle, I have worked several jobs in schools and I have seen firsthand the busy lives kids and teens lead. Many have sports, whether they are school sports or a traveling team. Some children do both. There are choir concerts, recitals, plays, and many other school-sponsored events. There is also homework and it is becoming increasingly common for the kids to have several hours of homework every night. Then, as they grow older, children will also begin to add social lives to everything else as they begin dating, going to movies and parties, and spending more time with their friends. Because of all this busyness, children receive messages about who they are from multiple sources. Even involved parents can get lost in the shuffle and the barrage of influences from friends, music, school, sports, and television can drown out their voices. Don't let yourself be drowned out. It is vitally important to spend time with your children and to maintain an influence in their lives.

I know that when I was growing up, my mother didn't have a lot of time to devote to me. She had seven children she was trying to raise and support, often without the help of a husband. As a result, I was forced to look elsewhere for love and attention, but even as I became involved in drugs and got into trouble at school, I still craved something from my parents: a hug, a kind word, anything that would let me know they loved me and cared for me. When my eighth-grade English teacher showed even the slightest interest in my life, I took that opportunity and clung to it for all I was worth. Her love made such a difference in my life that I later moved halfway across the country just to be in the same area as her because I knew she would be there for me.

Parents, I know you love your children. You want the very best for them and you are willing to do almost anything to see them grow up with better lives than you had. You want them to live out their dreams and you try to help them in any way you can. Even though they may not always say it, most children dream of just spending time with their parents.

Love isn't always buying new toys and clothes for them. Love isn't always making sure they are the top athlete, the best student, or the most popular in their class. Love isn't always making sure they succeed in absolutely everything they do. Sometimes love is just holding your children. Sometimes love is just talking with them. Sometimes love is laughing and crying together. Sometimes love is taking a moment to slow down and simply spending time with your children.

When you love with time, you send a message to your children. You tell them it is they who are most important—not getting the A, not winning the championship, not getting a music scholarship, but that *they*, no matter what they do, whether they succeed or fail, are important and that *they* are truly loved. When children see and realize their worth by the love of their parents, it gives them a solid foundation in their lives and a confidence to go out and accomplish their dreams.

Part of spending time with your children is finding out who they really are, what they like and dislike, and who they want to become. It is very easy for parents to impose their own hopes and desires on their children as far as careers and life goals are concerned, but I want to persuade you not to put too much pressure on your children in those areas. Even though it may be hard, encourage them to develop their own hobbies, their own interests, and their own passions and support them as they pursue those things.

At times, what your children find as their passion could be different than what you had imagined for their future. It is here that perhaps many parents begin to wonder if their children have homosexual tendencies. For instance, if a girl develops an interest in sports or cars or if a boy begins to pursue theatre and the arts, parents see that their children are interested in things not typically associated with their gender, at least according to the way society at large has defined gender roles. But are these the beginning of homosexual tendencies?

Society has tried to make it seem as if interest in certain activities is a precursor to homosexuality, but there is nothing inherently lesbian about women in sports and there is nothing inherently gay about men in the arts. If your children are interested in those activities, I would encourage you to let them pursue them. Try to take an interest in their interests. Be active in their lives, even if you don't share the same passion.

In many ways, I believe that homosexuality is a search for love and acceptance. When parents affirm their children's pursuits, even if it is only watching a game or a play, it gives the child a foundation of security and confidence. If children know they already have approval and love from their parents, they will be less likely to search for acceptance in things like drugs, alcohol, or homosexuality. My mother only came to a few of my basketball games, even though I played in both high school and college, and I think if she would have been able to be more involved in my life, things may have turned out differently for me.

Communication is also important. Sit your daughter down and ask her why she likes to play sports. Ask your son what aspects of art appeal to him. Their answers may surprise you and you may find out something about them you never knew before. However, if you don't have a history of talking with your children, it may be difficult to suddenly begin a conversation. It is important to let your children know from an early age that they can trust you with their hearts, with their fears, and with their dreams. Let them know they can come to you with any situation that may come up, but also ask them questions about their lives. While at times they may think you ask too many questions, secretly they will be glad that you care enough to ask about who they are with and where they are going.

Another important aspect of communication with your children is what you say to them. My mother and family constantly yelled at me about being too masculine. I was told to act more feminine because they didn't want me to grow up to be a lesbian. While I know my family was trying to help me, their words actually did the opposite. I was told I was like a little boy so many times that I began to believe it myself. It became my identity and I continued to act masculine, trying to become even tougher and stronger. If someone would have taken the time to ask why I liked to be tough, they may have found out that it was the only way I thought I could protect myself from being hurt.

It is not only the words you say to your children that matter, but also the way you say them. Find ways to affirm your children instead of pointing out negative things about their personality. If I had been encouraged when I did feminine activities rather than yelled at for doing masculine things, I would have found it much easier to be feminine. And again, parents, here is an area where you can lead best by example, by exhibiting the traits and qualities you want your children to have by the way you live your own life.

Take great care in finding out with whom your children spend time and who you allow to influence their lives. This includes both family and friends. I was abused by my stepfather as a young girl, and I know many of my homosexual friends had also been abused as children. Even if a child is raised in the most caring and loving home in the world, abuse by a family member or a close family friend will change their lives forever. Any type of abuse, whether it is sexual, physical, emotional, or verbal, will have lasting effects on the life of any child.

It would be ridiculous to say that every abused child will grow up to have homosexual tendencies. Abuse takes many different forms and its effects are different in every life it stains. Regardless of whether the effect of abuse will or could result in a willingness to engage in homosexual activities later in life, abuse should be prevented at all costs. If there is any sign that your children are being abused, remove them from the situation immediately and completely.

Abuse is not the only factor that could contribute to later homosexual tendencies; there are other influences as well. Sexual experimentation is being encouraged in schools, and at increasingly younger ages. Homosexuality is being taught as a viable lifestyle option and young children are taught that as long as they take care to have safe sex, any type of sex is acceptable. This is often done without parents being fully aware of the curriculum, which may be in direct contradiction to their moral beliefs and desires for their children's education. Parents, whether it concerns homosexuality or not, it is important to find out what your children are being taught in school.

Children are also taught by their exposure to various media. It is becoming harder to find movies, television shows, books, and music that promote family values. A large majority of modern media features premarital or abnormal sexual relationships, profanity, violence, and vague moral guidelines. This has expanded in recent years to include the acceptance and normalization of the homosexual lifestyle. Closely watch the media your children experience, especially younger children, because the lessons they learn watching the television may not be the lessons you want them to learn.

One of the biggest problems I think parents are facing and will face is their children's access to the Internet. Since its rapid explosion in the early nineties, the Internet has provided a mostly uncensored gateway to pornography and other immoral things children should not be allowed to experience. Exposure to pornography at a young age can create devastating consequences for children resulting in early sexual experimentation, sexual addictions, exposure to online sexual predators, unrealistic views of men and women, warped views of relationships, willingness to engage in homosexual behavior, objectification of both genders, intimacy issues, and sexual deviancy, to name a few.

Pre-kindergarten children know how to use computers and the Internet and literacy only increases the child's ability to navigate Web sites. There are software filters that can reduce the number and type of sites your child can access, but no filter is foolproof. The Internet can be a dangerous place. Make every effort to be at home when your children are using the Internet and to limit their unsupervised access. I also highly recommend keeping a personal computer out of your child's bedroom.

Peers also have an enormous influence on children. Who are your children's friends? How have they been raised? What type of things do they say or do? The old saying, "Show me your friends and I will show you your future," is still very true. When I was a child, there were a few girls on our street who eventually became lesbians. I remember my mother warning me about them, but I still felt curious about what made them different.

I am certainly not saying my early acquaintances caused me to later turn to homosexuality, but they may have been a factor. At the very least, they caused me to think about homosexuality in a way I would not have before. In the same way, your children's friends can have an impact on your children, and while it may not concern homosexuality, friends can influence your children to try alcohol, drugs, pornography, sex, smoking, or any number of other things.

Parents, it is okay to say no to your children. In fact, it can be downright healthy, both for them and for you. When you set up boundaries for them, you aren't holding them back, you are helping them learn the value of patience and you are also protecting them. Your children cannot always see or know what is best for themselves and so it isn't always good to give them whatever they want. It's okay to tell them they can't go to a movie, watch television, play on the computer, or visit a friend. It's okay to make them finish their homework before they go out with their friends. It's okay to say they can't play in school soccer *and* three traveling soccer leagues at the same time. Perhaps you can use the time they would be doing something else to get to know each other better.

While I have said much in this chapter, both about marriage and family, it isn't possible to protect your children from every bad influence or everything that could possibly cause them harm. There is no surefire way to ensure that your children will grow up exactly the way you want. As they grow older, you will eventually have to let them stand on their own two feet and begin walking, both literally and figuratively. The best that you, as a parent, will be able to do is to love them and teach them how to distinguish what is right from what is wrong. The best you can do is to lead them to a personal relationship with Jesus Christ. He loves them far more than you ever could, and therefore He will watch over them better than you will ever be able.

Psalm 127:3 says, "Sons are a heritage from the Lord, children are a reward from Him." Parenting is an incredible responsibility, but it is also a gift. In the midst of your obligations as a parent, don't forget to enjoy your children because they grow up all too quickly.

Chapter 10

FOR FRIENDS AND FAMILY

W HEN GOD CALLS, HE CALLS IN LOVE. HE LOVES everyone no matter who they are, where they have been, or what they have done. He loves each and every person and He died to rescue us all from sin. As His children, we are also supposed to love everyone just as He does, but that is much easier said than done. How are we supposed to love someone with whom we have nothing in common? How can we love those who live lifestyles that are in direct contrast to the way we live and believe?

In this chapter, I would like to talk about what we should do and how we can love when we are presented with the homosexuality of a family member, friend, or co-worker. When an individual announces their homosexuality, it can be a very tense time for both them and their loved ones. Relationships can be strained or broken and lifelong hurts can develop. If most of the relationships in their lives are thought lost, many homosexuals will turn to and embrace the homosexual community, which they believe is the only place left they can turn to for love and acceptance. My dearest friends, this should not be, either in perception or reality.

People often ask me what they should do when a loved one reveals their homosexuality. While there are certainly some things I will suggest, what most people usually mean when they ask me that is, How can I turn my loved one back into a heterosexual? My answer? *You* can't.

If someone you love or know has told you about their homosexuality, it has probably taken them a long time to gather up enough courage to share that information with you. Chances are they are more than a little nervous, fearful of outright rejection, instant condemnation, and intense loathing on the part of those they are telling. Sadly, sometimes their worst fears are confirmed by the reactions of those they love.

The initial announcement of homosexuality can be quite a shock to friends and family, especially if it is unexpected. Questions and comments can fly in those conversations and not all of them will be kind:

- Where is this coming from?
- How do you know you're gay?
- What did we do wrong?
- Does this mean you're attracted to me?
- How long have you known?
- Have you ever tried not being gay?
- How could you do this to us?
- Is this just an experimental phase?
- Don't you know homosexuals go to hell?
- What on Earth are you thinking?

I offer this advice to anyone who may have a loved one come to them and announce their homosexuality: stay calm when they tell you and remember that, despite their announcement, your loved one is still your loved one. It may be hard and come as a surprise, but yelling and saying hurtful things will not help you keep a meaningful relationship with them in any way. It is natural and appropriate to react to such news and to ask questions, but try to do so in a way that will keep your relationship with them intact.

I do not believe that excommunication from a family or a group of friends is ever helpful to someone struggling with homosexuality. Someone who has recently revealed their homosexuality is entering an unknown phase of their life and rejection from family and friends can cause them to totally abandon everything in order to search for someone or some place that will accept them. If they do leave everyone and everything behind, it will be just that much harder for them to come back, if they ever do.

It is important to know that you *cannot* change someone back into a heterosexual. You will never be able to force someone to do something they don't want to do or to be someone they don't what to be; you will only drive them further away. If they do return to heterosexuality, the decision has to be *theirs*, not yours. It has to be *their* desire, *their* heart, and *their* conviction or it will not work.

You will not be able to argue someone out of homosexuality. If you expect to say something so profound that a gay or lesbian will immediately leave homosexuality, prepare yourself for an argument and a lot of hurt feelings. It is important to communicate what you believe and that can be useful, but remember, if your loved one ever does leave homosexuality, your actions will have far more impact than your words.

So, what *do* you do when a loved one announces their homosexuality? I can give you no guarantees. I can only tell you what I think would be most helpful. Beyond your initial reaction, I believe three things are important: prayer, communication, and love.

Prayer is powerful. God wants us to come to Him with everything, including our concerns for others. Pray for your loved one, that God will protect them from bad influences and keep them safe. Pray they will be able to find a meaningful and personal relationship with God. Pray for yourself and those around you, that you will all be able to find ways to love and communicate with your loved one that will inspire greater and deeper faith in God. And finally, don't give up. Some prayers may take time, even years, before we see the results. The answer to your prayers may not always be what you expected, but remember that God is faithful and He loves you.

Do your best to keep lines of communication open with your loved one. I think it is important to let them know how you feel about their homosexuality and if you believe they are making the wrong decision, tell them. However, take care to separate the act from the individual. The words you say to them and the way you act toward them will echo in their minds for a long time. If you do tell them you think they are choosing a spiritually and physically dangerous lifestyle, present it in such a way that will let your loved one know you are rejecting their choice, but not them as an individual.

It is okay to remind your loved one of your own beliefs about homosexuality from time to time, but be careful that it is not the only thing you ever talk about. If you open each conversation with, "So, are you still gay?" you will find your relationship quickly unraveling. Likewise, constantly quoting Bible verses that talk about homosexuality may not be the best way to keep them talking to you. You don't have to hide your faith or your beliefs, and I am not in any way suggesting you should do that, but it is far better to *be* a living Bible by the way you treat them.

Rather than focusing specifically on your loved one's homosexuality, I would suggest getting to know them better.

Find out why they feel they are different. Talk about their past and current situations and also share things from your life. From my own experience and from having talked with others, I have found that homosexuality can often be a reaction to deep hurts in the past. By addressing some of the things from their past, it may be possible to get to the issues that are at the root of their reason for trying homosexuality; having someone to talk to about those things can be a relief. It may take some time, but I think the process of mutual sharing will help heal some of the hurts they have experienced.

If you can build a level of trust with your loved one so they know they can come to you with anything, no matter how bad or painful, you will have the opportunity to help them heal. Again, it may take some time. Sometimes it may seem as if they will never return or that they only return when they are at the lowest point in their life, but don't give up hope. Always point them back to God because He is the only One who can heal our hurts and He is the only One who can fill the emptiness in our hearts.

The best way you can point your loved one to God is to love them. Show them, not only by what you say, but also by what you do, that you care for them and that what happens in their life truly matters to you.

One of the reasons there are so many broken relationships between homosexuals and their families and between homosexuals and their churches is because some members of our society believe that a homosexual is somehow less than a person. Nothing could be further from the truth. Just because someone is homosexual does not make them unlovable. Love them enough to find out who they are as a person. Love them enough to have fun with them. Love them enough to become their friend. In doing so, you will find you are able to connect with them better and you will open up opportunities to minister to their needs.

If anything, I think that as churches, families, and friends, we need to be more aggressive in our *love* toward homosexuals. By aggressive, I don't mean we should be overbearing, insistent, or pushy. Rather, I mean we need to seek out more ways to help meet the needs of homosexuals. I think we too often try to ignore what is happening around us when instead we should be opening our arms and doors to help the hurting. If we are able to minister to broken hearts and real world needs, the message of God's love and redemption will be more readily accepted by those whose lives have been touched.

There is another aspect of love that I have talked about before and it is called tough love. There is a difference between accepting an individual as a person and accepting their behavior. Homosexuality, by its nature, seeks to push boundaries. If you are close to someone who is involved in homosexuality, at some point you will be forced to come face-to-face with the type of behavior that is associated with that lifestyle. This moment could come in many different forms and will probably happen more than once, but the essence of it is this: you will have a decision to make.

You will have to decide whether or not your continued presence with your loved one in that particular situation is because of your support of them as a person or if it crosses over to an approval of their behavior. This is a delicate line to walk and it would be prudent to think about what you will do before the situation arises so you will not have to make a split-second decision. If you do decide you are going to leave or withdraw because you do not want to give your approval to their behavior, tell your loved one why you are leaving and make sure you emphasize it is because of their behavior and not because of them as a person that you are leaving.

There may also come a time when you are not able to do anything to help improve the situation of your loved one. I know from experience that there is a very ugly side to the homosexual lifestyle. I was often lonely and empty. I tried to find fulfillment in smoking, drugs, and relationship after relationship. I did things I never thought I would do and became someone I never thought I would become. I know that many of my gay and lesbian friends suffered through that same despair and loneliness and they also did things they never thought they would do. If your loved one is going through a time like that and won't let you or anyone else be near them, the only thing you can do is keep praying for them.

Until this point, I have spoken in generalities, but now I want to focus on some specific situations about which many people have asked me.

I would like to start with what to do when homosexuality arises within a family. Family problems and conflicts will be different than problems in any other group because you cannot choose those to whom you are related. You cannot simply stop being family members when something happens that you don't agree with and I certainly don't recommend trying.

If a son or daughter announces their homosexuality, the first reaction of many parents is to wonder what they did wrong. In the previous chapter, I talked about some of the factors that can contribute to the formation of homosexuality in children. It is possible that the child experienced one or more of the situations I described, which may have been a factor in their decision to pursue homosexuality. However, it is also possible that the child has reached their decision independent of anything the parents could have done.

As a parent, I would try my best to find out why my child feels they are homosexual. Again, this may take some time and you may have to begin a dialogue of trust that hasn't yet existed before they are willing to share their deepest secrets and hurts with you. I don't suggest trying to do it all on the first day. Take the time to do it right.

Fathers, your role is very important. It is often the father who rejects a confession of homosexuality and that rejection can push your child even further away. If you have a fractured or even just a distant relationship with your child, do everything in your power to begin repairing it immediately and keep working at it. A healthy relationship with a father will make an incredible difference in the life of a child, even if they have already reached adulthood.

Mothers, it won't be any easier for you to accept your child's homosexuality, but I offer the same advice to you that I gave to fathers. Also, if there is anything you can do to encourage a relationship between the father and child, take those steps. And, as always, both parents should be praying for their children.

Children can also be faced with a parent turning homosexual. Several of my partners had been married with children, and I know that the experience of divorce with the added radical change of relationship can be very traumatic and confusing for children. From a child's perspective, there is little that can be done for their parents because the situation is very much out of their control. If you are faced with the homosexuality of one of your parents, I urge you to be there for them as much as you can, love them, and most of all, pray for them.

One of the hardest situations to face and to deal with is when a spouse leaves the marriage to be with someone of the same sex. While this decision can be made because of an unhappy marriage or a distant or abusive spouse, it can also come as a complete surprise in the middle of a seemingly happy relationship. It becomes painfully obvious to the husband or wife left behind that they did not know their spouse as well as they thought they did. The departing spouse may have had curiosity about or attraction to the opposite sex long before they said their marriage vows.

If you are confronted with this situation and still wish to have a relationship with your husband or wife, I want to caution you. It may not be possible for the relationship to be repaired, no matter how much you want it to happen. In order for it to happen, your spouse must also want it to happen. It will take both spouses and it will also take time. If there were problems in your marriage before your spouse left, then you will also have to pay attention to those issues and solve them before you reunite. If you are both committed to trying to make it work again, I highly recommend seeking the help of a pastor or a marriage counselor.

If there are children from your marriage with a spouse who has left you to pursue homosexuality, try to gain custody, if you are able to do so. The change from a heterosexual family to a homosexual family can be devastating for children when they are already dealing with a divorce. Please note, however, that I am not advocating that the children never see their parent. I think that access issues should be decided on a situational basis, though I believe that the children should live with the heterosexual parent.

When an extended family member chooses to embrace homosexuality, other family situations can arise, especially if you have young children. Parents often ask me if they should expose their children to a homosexual family member. My answer to them is, "Pray about it and discuss it with your spouse."

I think that each family faced with such a situation needs to decide for themselves what their response will be. There are several things the parents should consider: Will allowing contact with your homosexual family member prematurely expose your child to homosexuality? Are your children old enough and mature enough to understand homosexuality? If you decide against exposure, what does taking such a stand accomplish? How would it affect the family?

No matter what you decide, I think it is important for you to talk to your children about homosexuality as soon as you think they are old enough to understand it. You won't be able to shelter them from the family situation forever, so it is best to deal with it as early as possible. When you talk to your children, be careful not to minimize the effect of homosexuality, but do not glorify it either.

If you do allow contact between your children and your homosexual family member, talk with your family member beforehand about how you feel and what you consider appropriate behavior and conversation in front of your children. However, be sure to also be consistent and apply the same standards of conduct to heterosexual family members. And again, whenever possible, supervise your children when they are with others.

Beyond family members, we are often faced with friends or coworkers who are homosexual. Many times, if the friend or coworker is fairly public about their homosexuality, they will invite others to recognize their relationship with a commitment ceremony or through housewarming parties or some other social situation. This will often put those who do not agree with homosexuality in an awkward position.

I wish I could give a concrete answer about what to do in these situations, but again, I feel it is up to the individual to decide. If you are put in this situation, pray about it and consider carefully whether or not going to such a ceremony or party is honoring your friendship or condoning your friend's behavior.

With any situation in which you are confronted with the homosexuality of a family member or friend, please take the time to consider your reaction and the way you treat them. Proverbs 15:1, 28 says, "A gentle answer turns away wrath, but a harsh word stirs up anger.... the heart of the righteous weighs its answers, but the mouth of the wicked gushes evil."

Jude 17–25 sums up everything I have said in this chapter quite well:

> Dear friends, remember what the apostles of our Lord Jesus Christ foretold. They said to you, "In the last times there will be scoffers who will follow their own ungodly desires." These are men who divide you, who follow mere natural instincts and do not have the Spirit.
>
> But you, dear friends, build yourselves up in your most holy faith and pray in the Holy Spirit. Keep yourselves in God's love as you wait for the mercy of our Lord Jesus Christ to bring you to eternal life.
>
> Be merciful to those who doubt; snatch others from the fire and save them; to others show mercy, mixed with fear—hating even the clothing stained by corrupted flesh.
>
> To him who is able to keep you from falling and to present you before his glorious presence without fault and with great joy—to the only God and Savior be glory, majesty, power and authority, through Jesus Christ our Lord, before all ages, now and forevermore! Amen.

Chapter 11

WHAT CAN WE DO?

WHEN GOD CALLS, HE CALLS IN LOVE. HE HAS given us the family as the cornerstone of society as an extension of that love, so we can be nurtured and grow into adults in a healthy and safe environment. However, when we begin to change the family structure God gave us, we change the society that is based upon it.

In this chapter, I want to talk about how ideas have consequences. Marriage and family are pillars of our society and yet, in recent years, we have begun to alter their very structure through the way we live our lives, the way we educate our children, the way marriage and family are portrayed in the media, and in the laws that have protected their integrity.

Marriage and family are very closely related to sexuality. In fact, marriage protects sexuality and allows it to flourish, and when it flourishes, it becomes a family. When a marriage is healthy and stable, the family is also usually healthy and stable. There are always crises, arguments, and unusual situations that occur, but a healthy family is structured so it can work together and deal with most issues that arise.

A healthy family includes a mother and a father who are committed to each other in a loving, lifelong, and monogamous marriage. The lifelong commitment will offer stability for the children and will give them a foundation of confidence they will be able to use for the rest of their lives. Likewise, both the father and mother offer unique traits, behaviors, and character qualities that they pass on to their children by example and through direct instruction. While some of these qualities are shared between both parents, others can only be demonstrated by their respective gender.

Whereas a healthy family gives a child a framework from which they can build their life, an unhealthy family can only offer an incomplete outline. In some cases, the unhealthy foundation is not only incomplete but also damaging to the child. Sadly, we are seeing more and more examples of unhealthy families in our nation today. Teen pregnancy, extra-marital affairs, divorces, child and spousal abuse, rape, and incest all damage the families and the family members who experience those tragedies. If left unchecked, the family will grow more fractured and dysfunctional with each passing generation.

I spoke in previous chapters about how family life can impact a child's development, their sexuality, and how they interact with society, but now I want to talk about how education, media, and government have been affecting marriage and family.

I believe parents need to take the responsibility, no matter how uncomfortable it might be, to teach their own children about gender roles, gender interaction, sexual ethics, the act of sex itself, and the responsibilities and repercussions that result when they become intimate with another person. I do not believe that the best way to teach your children about sex is to have someone else teach them.

Unfortunately, parents have largely handed their responsibilities over to the schools. Our educators have decided that the best place to teach children about their sexuality is in the classroom and now nearly every child undergoes sexual education classes before they reach adolescence.

Many people will argue that if parents aren't willing or are too uncomfortable to teach their children about sex, someone should. Well then, if children must be taught about sex, what is being taught?

In comprehensive sex education, students are routinely taught the biological facts of how their bodies are meant to fit together. They are also taught about various sexually transmitted diseases, warned about the possibility of pregnancy, and instructed how to practice safe sex by using various contraceptives. Condoms are usually handed out and the students are encouraged to practice safe sex if they choose to experiment.

Does this all sound harmless? Let's take a closer look. By warning about possible consequences from sexual activity, but by not setting any firm boundaries, the message students receive is that they can experiment with whatever makes them feel good as long as nothing bad happens. If we teach teens how to use their sexuality, but then fail to teach them how to control it and to protect it within the confines of marriage, we are really not helping them.

Handing out condoms to teenagers in case they want to experiment is a little like handing out loaded guns in schools and telling the students how to use the safety without teaching them the responsibility of when, where, and how they should safely use the gun. As in the case of condoms, the gun can backfire. Condoms can break during sex and they are no guarantee to prevent conception or the transmission of STDs. The only way to truly prevent STDs or pregnancy is abstinence.

In some school districts, abstinence is taught simply as a birth control option. Teens also need to be taught *why* they should abstain. Reducing the number of STDs and teen pregnancies is good, but it doesn't really tell the teens why they should save themselves for marriage.

Many sex education programs don't emphasize how marriage is meant to protect and nourish a healthy sexuality. Teens aren't presented with examples of healthy marriages, so they have no reason to believe marriage is either desirable or worthwhile. Because they have many examples in their lives and in the lives of their classmates of families that don't work, many teens decide that perhaps marriage is something that is no longer applicable in today's society. It is truly a case of several bad apples spoiling the whole bunch, and it grows worse with each generation.

Healthy marriage and family examples should be taught and exemplified starting in the home, but they should also be reinforced by schools. I encourage schools to bring older married couples into the classroom to talk about how to have a successful marriage. Let them talk about the secrets to a good marriage, about how to resolve conflicts, what it's like to have children and to grow old together, and how fulfilling it can be to be committed to the same person for the rest of your life. Give teenagers positive examples and role models to aspire to and emulate instead of just trying to scare them with STDs and pregnancy or enabling irresponsible sexual behavior by handing out contraceptives.

Although I will talk more extensively about homosexuality in schools in the next chapter, I will touch on it briefly here. Homosexuality is present in education in increasing amounts, and it isn't limited to just the sexual education curriculum. The homosexual worldview often is integrated into everyday classroom activities in all subjects, sometimes through math word problems or assigned literature. Schools have also allowed homosexual groups to speak to classes or assemblies and to establish homosexual student clubs. The more students are exposed to homosexuality and told that it is an acceptable lifestyle option, the more willing they will be to try it.

The media also plays a major role in affecting the family in the way sexuality, marriage, and family life are portrayed. Positive role models are few and far between and negative examples are both normalized and glorified. Familial responsibilities and the consequences of "sexual freedom" are downplayed while sexuality without boundaries is portrayed as ideal and carefree. How can our society and our families be any greater than the heroes we put before us?

I must emphasize once again that ideas have consequences. The media has offered many unhealthy ideas to our families and children. The more those messages are received and applied to everyday life, the more damage is done to the family. Sex outside marriage is a near constant theme within today's media, but rarely is the ugly side shown, the side that shows the fatherless homes, the unwanted pregnancies, the sexually transmitted diseases, and the emotional harm that results from sleeping with multiple partners. The consequences of such irresponsible media result in a large number of the population seeking the glamour and excitement of sex outside marriage and finding themselves facing unexpected and potential life-ruining situations.

Through the media, we have been teaching our young girls that they need to weigh around one hundred pounds in order to be attractive to the opposite sex. The eating disorders and self-esteem issues that stem from this twisted idea are many and I have a feeling the problem is far more widespread than we realize. We have also taught our teen girls that they have to sleep with their boyfriends in order to be loved. Single motherhood has somehow now become a feminist ideal, but very few girls realize exactly how hard their lives are going to be because of it. At the same time, they are also encouraged to pursue careers at the cost of everything else.

Our teen boys are faring no better. They are taught a "safe" masculinity, one that strips them of many of the tools they are supposed to use to deal with the world. They are no longer the protectors and providers of their homes. Because their instinctual role has been taken away, they wander through life, wondering what to do and struggling to cope. They are taught that they don't have to be responsible sexually and that their contribution to fatherhood should be minimal. The demasculinization of our boys and men because of fatherless homes and media influences is growing and it will continue to have a negative impact on our families and society.

The media certainly doesn't do homosexuals or homosexuality any favors either. The ugly, lonely nature of homosexuality is never shown and the way homosexuals *are* portrayed is ridiculous. Far too often, the homosexual in the media is reduced to a punch line. The stereotypes have become a lesbian with short hair and a tough exterior, an artsy gay man with a lisp and a witty sense of humor, and a beautiful woman who is more than willing to experiment with bisexuality. It's time the media stops joking about homosexuality and begins to take a serious and honest look at the homosexual lifestyle.

What is an honest look? Let's look at some of the family situations that can influence the decision of teens and adults to enter homosexuality. Let's look at the search for fulfillment that drives the homosexual from one sexual relationship to the next. Let's look at the resulting dangers from such promiscuity. Let's look at the way HIV and AIDS destroy so many precious lives. Let's also stop ignoring stories of people who have decided to leave homosexuality.

In addition to looking at the real-life consequences of the ideas being advocated by the media, we also need to begin portraying good role models through the media. If you are reading this and work in the media industry or in a related field, I want to encourage and challenge you to show the benefits of a family staying together, of a father being involved in the lives of his children, of couples waiting until marriage for sex, and the amazing power of God to transform lives. If we set forth these examples and others like them, we will begin to see the deterioration of our marriages and families reverse.

The issue of what constitutes a healthy marriage relationship is not only ignored in the media, but also in our government. I will talk about this in more detail in the next chapter, but the definition of what a marriage is will have lasting impact on the future of our families and society. Although media and education are certainly getting their say, there are several legal fronts attempting to redefine marriage. One front is taking place in the judicial system, where some judges are allowing homosexuals to be issued marriage certificates. Another front is in the state and federal legislatures where the Defense of Marriage Acts (DOMA) define marriage as being between one man and one woman. They are being proposed as referenda to voters.

I certainly support DOMA efforts. In addition, our families, churches, and society should offer strong and stable family models. If traditional marriage and family continue to deteriorate, there is no doubt in my mind that both will be redefined forever. We must not only *defend* heterosexual marriage, we also need to *promote* it.

Promoting marriage should not only include providing good role models and talking about the benefits of marriage, but it should also include the enactment of pro-marriage and pro-family legislation. While I will leave the details of such legislation to those better qualified than myself, I believe it is past time to take an active approach to helping marriages and families stay together.

If helping to preserve marriage means that pastors and priests need to preach more about marriage and the importance of faithfulness from the pulpits, I say, preach it. If it means we need to bring married couples into our schools to talk to students about how to have successful marriages, I say open the doors wide. If it means that the media needs to start creating content that promotes marriage and family, I say create it and we will watch. If it means that our senators and representatives begin introducing legislation that benefits marriage and family, I say create the legislation and we will vote for it. Marriage and family are too important to the functioning of our society to simply let them fall apart.

I want to encourage you to live and act according to Philippians 4:8, which says, "Finally brothers, whatever is true, whatever is noble, whatever is right, whatever is pure, whatever is lovely, whatever is admirable—if anything is excellent or praiseworthy—think about such things." If we are able to apply these values to our marriages and families, built on a foundation of a relationship with Jesus Christ, they will grow strong and will not fall.

QUESTIONS AND ANSWERS

WHEN GOD CALLS, HE CALLS IN LOVE. WHEN He speaks to us, God talks in love through His Spirit, granting wisdom and knowledge to all who seek His heart. In this chapter, I am going to attempt to answer some commonly asked questions about homosexuality. Some of the questions are very difficult and complex, but I will do my best to answer them. I certainly don't claim to know everything about homosexuality; all I do know is what I have lived and what God has done in my life. Where I have been able to, I have gone to the Scriptures for my answers because I believe God's Word should be the first place we look when we need wisdom and it should also be the final authority in our lives.

What does *called out* mean?

I've used the term *called out* for several reasons. I believe it best describes the change that happened in my life. God was always present and by my side, calling my name even though I was trapped in sin. When I finally listened to that calling, it wasn't by my strength that I left the homosexual lifestyle; it was by God's grace alone. Left to myself, I could never have done it, but God sent the right people at the right times to help me find my way back to Him. He literally called me out of the homosexual lifestyle.

Called out has its origin in 1 Peter 2:9, which says, "But you are a chosen people, a royal priesthood, a holy nation, a people belonging to God, that you may declare the praises of him who called you out of darkness into his wonderful light."

Many homosexuals use the pop culture phrase "coming out of the closet" to describe when they publicly announce their homosexuality. To my knowledge, there is no phrase to describe someone who has publicly left homosexuality. I would like to suggest that an appropriate expression might be that they have been "called out into God's love."

Do you feel you were born homosexual?

Despite the current debate over whether or not people are born gay, I know I was not born homosexual. This is why: my early childhood was filled with sorrow, hardship, and verbal, physical, and sexual abuse. As a little girl, I was subjected to people telling me I looked and acted like a boy. I was constantly told not to become a lesbian like the neighbor girls. No one spoke words of encouragement into my life until it was too late. The power of words is enormous, especially at such a young and vital age of development. What people said began to take root and grow in my heart and I believe that, although they weren't the sole factor, the words of those around me paved the way to my eventual lesbianism.

I also believe my physical environment contributed to my later lifestyle choice. My mother was a strict, hard woman who didn't always know how to handle her children, even though I know she loved us. Her discipline was tough and physical and I literally dreaded it. My home life was always in turmoil. My real father took no interest in my life. The only father figure I had was an alcoholic. I was sexually abused by two different men. We were poor. I constantly got into fights. When I was thirteen, my family's house burned down.

These were all the lessons of my childhood and they taught me to become hard, strong, and bitter. I was far from the conventional image of femininity. After the sexual abuse, I hardened my heart even further and I had even more reason to hate and distrust men.

Even with everything that happened in my childhood, I became engaged to be married to a man years later. I had experienced homosexual urges and feelings before that point, but I had been rejected every time I had tried to make advances. In every case, a lesbian relationship failed to materialize until after I became engaged and Ruth began to show interest in me. When I recognized that the interest was mutual and began spending time with her, I didn't guard my thoughts or actions and I fell into a sexual relationship with her. That act marked a turning point in my life, one that led me down a fourteen-year road to lesbianism.

I was not born homosexual. I made a decision. My background and childhood may have been factors to influence that decision, but they did not take away my responsibility for making the decision. When I finally listened to God's call on my life, I made another decision, this time to leave homosexuality. There were many circumstances that led up to that decision as well, but I had to first be willing.

What about others who say they were born homosexual?

Based on my personal experience and the factors that contributed to my choosing to enter the homosexual lifestyle, I would at the very least have several questions to ask anyone who said they were born homosexual. I would ask them about their early childhood and about how they were treated by their parents, their siblings, their extended family, their friends, and any strangers in their lives.

For men, I would ask if their interests tended toward the arts or creative pursuits or toward anything other than the stereotypical boy's childhood of playing with trucks, guns, and sports. For women, I would ask if they also defied the traditional notion of what little girls are supposed to be like and instead took up sports or other activities usually more associated with their male counterparts. I would ask these things, not because there is anything inherently gay about arts or creativity, or lesbian about sports, but there is a wrong *perception* that they are activities that indicate future homosexuality.

To both men and women, I would ask if anyone ever compared them to the opposite sex. Did they suffer abuse in any way, whether verbal, emotional, physical, or sexual? What was their family life like? Did they have a father figure? Did they grow up in a single parent home? Did they have exposure to pornography at a young age? Did they have a traumatic break-up of a relationship as a teen or young adult? Did they experience a consistent example of love or were they constantly striving to gain the attention of their parents and elders?

There are so many different factors that contribute to who we are as individuals in general that I find it difficult to accept when someone simply states that they were born homosexual. When you consider that every experience shapes and molds us for good or bad, sometimes in ways we don't even notice or remember, the question of whether or not people are born gay suddenly becomes much more complicated. Our childhood years are formative, but few of us hold on to more than the few memories that stand out for good or bad. In some cases, bad memories can even be blocked out or repressed when they are too painful to keep experiencing them through remembrance. We sometimes also remember things that didn't happen or have memories that represent how we wish things had happened. Time has its way of erasing or dulling memories.

I must also draw attention to the fact that not every homosexual will claim they have been born gay. Although the homosexual community tries to downplay or ignore their existence, there are individuals such as myself who will attribute their homosexuality to a lifestyle choice.

There are also those individuals who claim to have been born gay, but inwardly feel as if their homosexuality was a choice and they simply use the "born gay" argument as a rationalization to justify a lifestyle choice they don't feel comfortable with. All of these factors should at least call into some question the statement that people are simply born gay.

Is there a gay gene?

In answering this question, I would like to take a moment to consider the implications of the search for a gay gene. Would the discovery of a gay gene legitimize the homosexual lifestyle? This question seems to be driving the research, but in my opinion, it doesn't really matter. There are already proven genetic factors that contribute to alcoholism, violent temperament, and an array of mental illnesses, all of which can lead to socially unacceptable and illegal behavior. The fact that people are born with such conditions does not give them the right to do whatever they want. Rather, they are expected, and in many cases helped, to overcome their genetic predispositions. If a discovery occurred proving the existence of a gay gene, I believe homosexuality should be considered in the same manner.

I am not a geneticist or scientist; I can only offer my layman's perspective concerning the search for a gay gene. What I understand is this: Since the 1990's, the search for the so-called gay gene has caught national headlines, but the search has been largely unsuccessful. To date, no single determining genetic factor has been found to cause homosexuality. In fact, there is far more evidence supporting environmental factors as a cause of homosexuality than genetic causes.

For any further information, I would direct the reader to the National Association for Research and Therapy of Homosexuality. Their website, http://www.narth.com, has resources available concerning studies about the genetic, environmental, and psychological causes of homosexuality.

Did God create people to be gay?

I believe it is best to turn to the Bible to properly answer this question. Let's start first with the story of Creation, which was God's blueprint for the world before the entrance of sin. Genesis 1:27–28 says, "So God created man in his own image, in the image of God he created him; male and female he created them. God blessed them and said to them, 'Be fruitful and increase in number; fill the earth and subdue it. Rule over the fish of the sea and the birds of the air and over every living creature that moves on the ground.'"

Heterosexual relationships were set as a precedent, according to the Creation account, and no mention was made of a homosexual union. Male and female is the only possible pairing that could allow mankind to be fruitful and multiply over the earth. The heterosexual model for relationships is mentioned throughout Scripture again and again as God's plan for marriage and family.

Jesus, in speaking of marriage and divorce to the Pharisees, said this in Matthew 19:4–5, "Haven't you read...that at the beginning the Creator 'made them male and female' and said, 'For this reason a man will leave his father and mother and be united to his wife, and the two will become one flesh'?

So they are no longer two, but one. Therefore, what God has joined together, let man not separate." The apostle Paul also reaffirms this in Ephesians 5:31, using the exact same wording. Both Jesus and Paul are promoting a heterosexual union through marriage. No mention is made of homosexual relationships and their absence speaks loudly that they were not a part of God's plan.

If God did not create homosexuality, where did it come from? The fall of mankind in the Garden of Eden started a cycle of sin that fed upon itself, growing progressively worse the more entrapped we became. Paul describes the process in Romans 1:20–32:

> For since the creation of the world God's invisible qualities—his eternal power and divine nature—have been clearly seen, being understood from what has been made, so that men are without excuse. For although they knew God, they neither glorified him as God nor gave thanks to him, but their thinking became futile and their foolish hearts were darkened. Although they claimed to be wise, they became fools and exchanged the glory of the immortal God for images made to look like mortal man and birds and animals and reptiles.
>
> Therefore God gave them over in the sinful desires of their hearts to sexual impurity for the degrading of their bodies with one another. They exchanged the truth of God for a lie, and worshiped and served created things rather than the Creator—who is forever praised. Amen.
>
> Because of this, God gave them over to shameful lusts. Even their women exchanged natural relations for unnatural ones. In the same way the men also abandoned natural relations with women and were inflamed with lust for one another. Men committed

indecent acts with other men and received in themselves the due penalty for their perversion.

Furthermore, since they did not think it worthwhile to retain the knowledge of God, he gave them over to a depraved mind, to do what ought not to be done. They have become filled with every kind of wickedness, evil, greed, and depravity. They are full of envy, murder, strife, deceit, and malice. They are gossips, slanderers, God-haters, insolent, arrogant, and boastful; they invent ways of doing evil; they disobey their parents; they are senseless, faithless, heartless, ruthless. Although they know God's righteous decree that those who do such things deserve death, they not only continue to do these very things but also approve of those who practice them.

According to this passage of Scripture, homosexuality came about because of the persistence of mankind in its sin. Individuals sought to replace the natural union God had created between man and woman with unnatural ones. God allowed it because they had already rejected Him in their hearts. He would not force them to love Him and so He gave them over to their sins, even though the consequence of sin is death.

But God did not abandon mankind to sin. His love for us wouldn't allow it. He sent His perfect Son to earth to suffer the death that should have been ours, taking our place. Because of Jesus' sacrifice, Romans 10:9 says, "If you confess with your mouth that 'Jesus is Lord,' and believe in your heart that God raised Him from the dead, you will be saved." Now anyone, whether homosexual, murderer, adulterer, thief, liar, or any other kind of sinner can approach the throne of God and be forgiven for their sins by believing in the name of Jesus. God did not create people to be gay; He created them to be free from sin.

Is homosexuality a sin and if so, what is the basis?

The Bible states several times that homosexual acts are not to be practiced. When God gave Moses sexual codes of conduct, He said in Leviticus 18:22, "Do not lie with a man as one lies with a woman; that is detestable." The command is given again several chapters later in Leviticus 20:13, "If a man lies with a man as one lies with a woman, both of them have done what is detestable. They must be put to death; their blood will be on their own heads." Romans 1:26–27 also says, "Because of this, God gave them over to shameful lusts. Even their women exchanged natural relations for unnatural ones. In the same way the men also abandoned natural relations with women and were inflamed with lust for one another. Men committed indecent acts with other men, and received in themselves the due penalty for their perversion."

According to the verses above, God does not approve of homosexual acts and instead has hard consequences for those who commit them. Homosexuality is called detestable, shameful, unnatural, indecent, and a perversion; in short: sin.

There is also the case of the cities of Sodom and Gomorrah, which Genesis 19 tells us were destroyed by burning sulfur because of their wickedness. Many gay activists will claim that the sin committed by these two cities was inhospitality, but the Scripture reveals a much more wicked situation.

Genesis 19:4–6 says this after two angels came to the house of Lot, Abraham's nephew living in Sodom, "Before they had gone to bed, all the men from every part of the city of Sodom—both young and old—surrounded the house. They called to Lot, 'Where are the men who came to you tonight? Bring them out to us so that we can have sex with them.' Lot went outside to meet them and shut the door behind him and said, 'No, my friends. Don't do this wicked thing.'"

While it certainly may have been inhospitable for the men of Sodom to want to rape Lot's guests, "inhospitable" does not begin to cover their sinful desires or actions. Sodom may have had many other sins, but these verses make the extent of their sexual perversion very clear. It was referred to as wicked and God dealt with it by issuing severe consequences.

Some argue that since Jesus doesn't mention homosexuality, it isn't a sin. However, as was mentioned in the previous question, Jesus taught that marriage is to be between a man and a woman. He reaffirmed the heterosexual model that is found throughout the Bible and He promoted it to the exclusion of all other lifestyles.

The argument that scriptures that speak about homosexuality can be dismissed because they are no longer culturally relevant falls apart when one considers that those scriptures were written some fifteen hundred years apart and in vastly different cultures. God's law transcends time and culture and His commandments concerning homosexuality are no less relevant in the twenty-first century than they were in the times of Moses and Paul.

Is homosexuality a choice?

In answering this question, I would like to take apart the term *homosexuality*, because I believe there are several important distinctions to be made. There is a difference between homosexual inclination and homosexual behavior.

As I have stated previously, I believe much of my own willingness to experiment with homosexuality was influenced by the environment in which I grew up. I was hardened by a difficult childhood and the men in my life abused me and treated me as an object. Naturally, I tried to limit getting hurt again and, because so many men had hurt me, I began to gravitate toward relationships with women. The relationships I was looking for weren't necessarily sexual; I was looking more for emotional acceptance, but over time I started craving the sexual aspect of it as well.

Now, I certainly didn't choose to be abused, sexually or physically. I didn't choose not to have a father figure. I didn't choose to be hurt by men. I didn't choose to have people tell me that I looked like a boy or call me a lesbian. There were so many things in my life I didn't choose and, in many ways, I think my homosexual inclinations and my drug addictions were natural reactions to the horrible hand life had dealt me.

It would be a misrepresentation to lay the entire blame of my homosexual inclinations on my childhood. I also fed my desire by placing myself in compromising positions and in the way of temptation. A desire was created and it grew, constantly demanding more and more for its fulfillment. James 1:14–15 says, "Each one is tempted, when, by his own evil desire, he is dragged away and enticed. Then, after desire has conceived, it gives birth to sin, and sin, when it is full grown, gives birth to death." I experienced a type of death over and over again as I sought to fill the emptiness in my life with things that could never satisfy. In the end, only Christ was able to bring me back to life.

Homosexual behavior, however, is something completely different from homosexual inclination in that it is entirely based on choice. When I left my fiancé Laurence and began a sexual relationship with Ruth, it was a decision on my part, a choice. Ruth did not force me to have sex with her; it was something I did willingly. Engaging in homosexual behavior, just the same as engaging in extra-marital heterosexual activities, has always been and will always be a choice.

Obviously my homosexual inclinations made it easier for me to fall into a sexual relationship with another woman, but it is something I could have avoided. I spent so much time with Ruth and became so emotionally involved that even Laurence pointed it out to me. I could have ended my relationship with Ruth or, at the very least, limited the time I spent with her. I failed to realize the temptation I was playing with and I fell into sin.

Homosexual behavior can be controlled, but just like heterosexual sex, once you begin it becomes very difficult to stop. I was only able to stop by giving my life to God and opening myself to accountability with the women in my Bible study. I had to leave the situations that caused me to be tempted to return to the lifestyle I had left behind. It was a struggle, and I sometimes fought to go back to what I had left behind, but God was faithful and He gave me the strength and grace to overcome my temptations. I know the same power and grace is available for all who call on the name of the Lord.

Can a Christian be gay?

This is a very difficult question to answer and it could and should be expanded to, "Can a Christian continuously live in sin?" Homosexuality, like any sin, separates us from God, for He cannot tolerate sin in His presence. God is always willing to forgive us when we ask, but what happens when we refuse to learn from our mistakes, when we continually return to the same sin?

Jesus had this to say in Matthew 7:18–23:

> A good tree cannot bear bad fruit, and a bad tree cannot bear good fruit. Every tree that does not bear

good fruit is cut down and thrown into the fire. Thus, by their fruit, you will recognize them.

Not everyone who says to me, "Lord, Lord," will enter the kingdom of heaven, but only he who does the will of my Father who is in heaven. Many will say to me on that day, "Lord, Lord, did we not prophesy in your name, and in your name drive out demons and perform many miracles?" Then I will tell them plainly, "I never knew you. Away from me, you evil doers!"

It is clearly taught in Scripture that we are saved through faith in Jesus Christ and that faith is confirmed by what we say and do. It is not enough to merely say you believe in God; you must also obey what He has set forth in His Word. James 2:19, 24 says, "You believe that there is one God. Good! Even the demons believe that—and shudder...a person is justified by what he does and not by faith alone."

When we accept Jesus Christ as our Lord and Savior, we enter into a new life. We ought to willingly place ourselves beneath the authority of Scripture and accept the Holy Spirit as our inner voice. As a part of that process, our lives begin to change. Mine did. It wasn't instantaneous, and it definitely wasn't easy, but my life has begun to bear fruit because of my obedience to God.

In answering the question of whether or not a Christian can be gay, I want to point something out. There is a difference between being tempted with homosexuality and giving into that temptation. Can a Christian be tempted with homosexuality? Can a Christian be tempted with any sin? Certainly. The temptation itself is not the sin; it is the surrender to that temptation that separates us from God. We do not have to give into temptation. First Corinthians 10:13 says, "No temptation has overtaken you except such as is common to man; but God is faithful, who will not allow you to be tempted beyond what you are able, but with the temptation will always make the way of escape, that you may be able to bear it" (NKJV).

What should we do when tempted? Get out of that situation! The apostle Paul wrote in 2 Timothy 2:22, "Flee the evil desires of youth, and pursue righteousness, faith, love, and peace, along with those who call on the Lord out of a pure heart." By placing ourselves in the way of temptation, we are only setting ourselves up to sin. Why risk it?

If we do sin, we know there is forgiveness because of the blood of Jesus. But just because there is forgiveness, it does not mean we are given permission to do whatever we want. True repentance means we not only ask for forgiveness, but that we also turn away from our sins. If you lie, ask for forgiveness, but then do not go back to lying. If you steal, ask forgiveness, but then steal no more. If you sleep with a boyfriend or girlfriend, ask God to forgive you, but then stop sinning. If you engage in homosexual activity, seek forgiveness, but then repent and stop sinning.

Just as there is forgiveness for a Christian who lies and repents, so there is also forgiveness for a Christian who participates in homosexual activity and repents. But just because there is forgiveness for our sins, it does not mean our sins are without consequences. Adultery can result in a troubled marriage or divorce; theft can end in a prison sentence; many babies are born because of premarital sexual activity; and homosexual activity can bring about an array of identity issues as well as various physical consequences.

God gave us laws in Scripture for a reason: to protect us. While we may not always understand the reasons behind the rules, we need to accept them as God's truth. They were designed, not to enslave us, but to set us free from the bondage of sin. And once we profess Jesus Christ as our Lord and Savior, we are held to an even higher standard of following God's Word because we have been given the truth.

Now, for those who believe they can get away with a lifestyle of sin (whether it is murder, cheating, homosexual behavior, adultery, theft, or any other repeated sin) because of the grace and forgiveness of God, Scripture offers a very harsh warning in Hebrews 10:26–31:

> If we deliberately keep on sinning after we have received the knowledge of the truth, no sacrifice for sins is left, but only a fearful expectation of judgment and of raging fire that will consume the enemies of God. Anyone who rejected the Law of Moses died without mercy on the testimony of two or three witnesses. How much more severely do you think a man deserves to be punished who has trampled the Son of God under foot, who has treated as an unholy thing the blood of the covenant that sanctified him, and who has insulted the Spirit of grace? For we know Him who said, "It is mine to avenge; I will repay," and again, "The Lord will judge His people." It is a dreadful thing to fall into the hands of the living God.

First Corinthians 6:9–11 also says this:

> Do you not know that the wicked will not inherit the kingdom of God? Do not be deceived: Neither the sexually immoral nor idolaters nor adulterers nor male prostitutes nor homosexual offenders nor thieves nor the greedy nor drunkards nor slanderers nor swindlers will inherit the kingdom of God. And that is what some of you *were*. But you were washed, you were sanctified,

you were justified in the name of the Lord Jesus Christ
and by the Spirit of our God. (Emphasis added.)

Does this mean that God's love is false, if He punishes those who do not obey Him? No. God's love is never false, but He does not like to be mocked. Jesus died so we might live, a gift only God could give. He expects us to respect Him and to obey Him, and He has clearly warned us about what will happen if we do not.

Having said all of that, if you are a new believer in Christ, it may take a while to entirely leave behind the things you did before. I struggled and it took time. I still struggle in some areas. God's love transforms us, but He knows and understands that very few of us are able to change completely overnight. As we are able to handle it, He will give us the grace and strength to change.

What view should the church take on homosexuality?

The church needs to educate itself about homosexuality on many different levels. We need to discover and teach what Scripture says about homosexuality. We need to become aware of the advances of homosexual programs in schools, in churches, in politics, and in our culture and we need to counter them with sound scriptural doctrine as well as our own scientific research. We need to reemphasize the integrity of the family and the importance of our own spiritual lives. And finally, we need to find out how best to minister to the homosexual community.

The Bible clearly teaches that homosexuality is wrong, but many churches find themselves wavering on this issue. Why? As Christians, our allegiance is to God and His Word, not to whatever popular culture happens to think is right at the time. The Gospel of Christ includes the entire Bible, not just the parts that make us feel good, and that Gospel does not change.

The apostle Peter warned against false teachers and prophets, saying this in 2 Peter 2:17–21:

> These men are springs without water and mists driven by a storm. Blackest darkness is reserved for them. For they mouth empty, boastful words and, by appealing to the lustful desires of sinful human nature, they entice people who are just escaping from those who live in error. They promise them freedom, while they themselves are slaves of depravity—for a man is a slave to whatever has mastered him. If they have escaped the corruption of the world by knowing our Lord and Savior Jesus Christ and are again entangled in it and overcome, they are worse off at the end than they were at the beginning. It would have been better for them not to have known the way of righteousness, than to have known it and then turn their backs on the sacred command that was passed on to them.

Many churches today, instead of teaching what the Bible says about homosexuality, have decided to appeal to "the lustful desires of sinful human nature." In my own case, I very nearly made a decision to have a sex-change operation because a priest told me and my partner that what we were doing what was right in the eyes of God.

Church, there is no excuse for allowing sin in your midst. Christ is returning for a spotless bride—start acting like one!

Church, if you embrace homosexuality as a valid lifestyle choice, you are not helping anyone. Instead, you are actually hurting those who come to Christ and wish to escape the bondage of homosexuality. God has warned you in His Word, do not think there will not be consequences for your actions and teaching. You are refusing to acknowledge the full and transforming power of the Gospel and you are leading all who follow your teachings astray.

Too many churches today are afraid of offending people that visit because they are more concerned about the size of their congregations and the amount of money in their offering plates than they are about preaching God's Word. This compromise is not limited to homosexuality, but also includes adultery, premarital sex, pornography, and multiple areas that are considered by some to be too offensive to mention or take a stand on. Church, what has happened? Teach God's Word! If no one else will say it, I will—I am not ashamed of the Gospel of Jesus Christ.

We also cannot make the mistake of thinking that if we ignore the issue of homosexuality, it will just go away. It is here and it's not going anywhere. Our children are being taught in our schools that homosexuality is a valid lifestyle option. They are being encouraged to experiment sexually, whether it is with heterosexual, homosexual, bisexual, or transgender lifestyles. The lesson is being taught: whatever you think might make you feel good, try it.

The same is also being taught in some of our churches and it is being broadcast in nearly every television show, shown in almost every movie, and printed in many books. In addition, homosexual advocacy groups are pushing for legislation to be enacted that will seriously undermine the structure of the family in an effort to legitimize the homosexual lifestyle.

As the church, we need to educate ourselves about the homosexual worldview and counter it with the worldview God set forth in Scripture. We need to present a united body that holds to what the Bible says about homosexuality; that stands up in civic, cultural, and spiritual forums for what is right; and that is willing to extend open arms of love to the homosexual community.

In addition to countering the homosexual worldview with Scripture, we also need to make use of other tools that are at our disposal. There are many Christian scientists, geneticists, researchers, psychiatrists, psychologists, and apologists who have much to contribute to the issues surrounding homosexuality, but have largely kept silent. I want to encourage you to add your voices and talents by contributing to a movement that will set people free from bondage.

One of the greatest things hindering the church from taking a stand against the legitimization of the homosexual lifestyle is its loss of any sort of moral authority. The church used to set itself apart from the world because it followed and taught the Word of God. Now, however, there is very little difference between the lifestyles and moral practices of the church and those of secular society.

Church, you were called to be pure and holy, set apart, in the world but not of it. Repent, remove the plank in your own eye before you speak to your brothers about the specks in their eyes. If we have been mocked and called hypocrites concerning our stance on homosexuality, it is rightly so. It is time for us to live lifestyles consistent with the Word of God. Stop cursing, complaining, cheating, lusting, lying, engaging in any sort of extra-marital sexual activity, and submit yourselves to God.

Only once we have begun to live as God would have us live will we be able to reach out to the homosexual community in love. Our churches need to become places of refuge for the hurting. Our homes need to become places of healing.

Our lives need to become living testimonies of the power and love of the almighty Creator of heaven and earth.

If we take a strong stand on homosexuality, we will come under fire. But, if at the same time, we also open ourselves up to accept with love anyone who will come to the altar of Christ, we will make a difference in many lives. There is a balance that must be found between countering homosexual culture and loving individuals struggling with homosexuality. If we err, let us err on the side of love.

"God hates gays," is never going to win anyone to Christ. It is a lie; God doesn't hate anyone. Rather, let our message be, "God so loved the world that He gave His one and only Son that whoever believes in Him will not perish but have everlasting life." When ministering to the homosexual community, their homosexuality should be a secondary issue. Yes, it is a sin, and the Bible says so, but all have sinned. The focus needs to be on God's love. Let us lead them to Christ and then let *His* power and *His* grace transform their lives. We can certainly be there to support, guide, and teach; but it is the Holy Spirit who must do the transforming work.

Should homosexuals be elected to leadership positions in the church?

The Bible gives very specific instruction on the requirements for leaders within the church and holds those in leadership to a higher standard than those they lead. While the criteria for every single leadership position in the church are not covered within Scripture, there is enough evidence to give us a clear picture. Consider what Paul said to young Timothy as he told him how overseers and deacons should conduct themselves in 1 Timothy 3:1–13:

Here is a trustworthy saying: If anyone sets his heart on being an overseer, he desires a noble task. Now the overseer must be above reproach, the husband of but one wife, temperate, self-controlled, respectable, hospitable, able to teach, not given to drunkenness, not violent but gentle, not quarrelsome, not a lover of money. He must manage his own family well and see that his children obey him with the proper respect. (If anyone does not know how to manage his own family, how can he take care of God's church?) He must not be a recent convert, or he may become conceited and fall under the same judgment as the devil. He must also have a good reputation with outsiders, so that he will not fall into disgrace and into the devil's trap.

Deacons, likewise, are to be men worthy of respect, sincere, not indulging in much wine, and not pursuing dishonest gain. They must keep hold of the deep truths of the faith with a clear conscience. They must first be tested; and then if there is nothing against them, let them serve as deacons.

In the same way, their wives are to be women worthy of respect, not malicious talkers but temperate and trustworthy in everything.

A deacon must be the husband of but one wife and must manage his children and his household well. Those who have served well gain an excellent standing and great assurance in their faith in Christ Jesus.

The above verses demonstrate that those in leadership are to be tested and should be able and willing to hold on to the deep truths of the faith while not violating any of them. While it is certainly not the deepest truth of Christianity, the Bible does teach that homosexuality is a sin. Living a homosexual lifestyle is in direct opposition to what Scripture teaches is an example of living above reproach, being self-controlled, and holding to the deep truths of the faith with a clear conscience.

If a leader of a church is involved in any repeated sin, whether it is adultery, homosexuality, fornication, theft, murder, or lying, the Bible makes a clear case for that leader to be removed from leadership.

What can the church do to help homosexuals?

Our job is not to make homosexuals straight. Rather, our job is to preach the gospel and make disciples of all nations. The greatest thing the church could possibly do for homosexuals is to bring them to the saving knowledge of Jesus Christ. Yes, homosexuality is a sin, but Christ died for sinners. His grace and His power are transforming; they leave no willing life unchanged. Let us let the Holy Spirit do His work.

Again and again, I must say this: our best and greatest hope to win the homosexual community and the world at large to Christ is for us to live consistent lives of love and righteousness. We must rid ourselves of the hypocrisy and unrighteousness that have been part of the church for far too long. We must turn our hearts back to Christ and our lives back to the way Scripture says we must live.

As a part of loving and reaching out to individuals, we need to realize that we cannot force anyone to change. When I was living as a lesbian, nothing anyone said to me about homosexuality was going to change me until I was ready. God was constantly calling to me the entire time, but He wasn't going to force me. I needed to want to change. I needed to see that there was nothing in the lesbian lifestyle that could fill the empty spot in my heart. It was only then that God was able to take my willing heart and begin to mold it after His own.

We must love, but it will help no one if we encourage them in their sin. Tolerance is fine and good, but tolerance does not mean that we must agree, nor does it mean we should let biblical morality be erased from our society. We must never tolerate sin or behavior that is unhealthy and harmful. The church must take a strong stand against the practices and agendas of the homosexual community while remaining loving toward individuals struggling with homosexuality.

Church, I believe with all my heart that if you open your doors, you will find opportunities to minister. Homosexuals are already knocking on your doors and sitting in your pews, seeking guidance, wisdom, acceptance, healing, and love. Unfortunately, they are either being turned away or encouraged in their sin far too often. I have heard horror stories of gays and lesbians going to churches for help only to be turned away, ashamed and alone.

If there is no healing to be found in our churches, where can people go? If the love of the body of Christ goes cold, we will have lost much more than a culture war, we will have lost the healing tie that binds us together, defines us, and sets us free. And if we do not have that, then we have nothing.

We need to find ways to help the willing, those who want to be free from their struggle with homosexuality. There are organizations, churches, and individuals who have faithfully ministered to gays and lesbians, leading them to Christ and helping them recover their sexuality, but there is more work to be done.

Homosexuality affects nearly every church and Christian in some way. There are few people today who do not come into contact with homosexual individuals, but many do not understand their family members, friends, or coworkers who are living such a different lifestyle than their own. The church needs to educate itself about homosexuality, its causes, its dangers, and its pain, as well as about how to reach out to those who struggle with homosexuality and want to be free.

How do we educate ourselves about homosexuality? Many churches don't know how to minister to homosexuals and so they do nothing. My suggestion is this: ask those who have left the homosexual lifestyle behind about what impacted them the most. Ask those ministries and individuals who have already reached out to homosexuals about what works. Churches can bring in guest speakers and have conferences that will educate their congregations about homosexuality. Pastors have opportunities every week to preach from their pulpits. Deacons, elders, and laypeople can have classes or teach studies.

For too long, too many in the church have been under the impression that homosexuality cannot be changed, that it is something to which an individual must simply give in. This is simply not true. My life is living proof and I know I am not alone. My story of leaving homosexuality is not unique—there are thousands of ex-gays—and now it is time to spread the word that there is another path, another option, another hope: Jesus Christ.

Beyond education, what more can churches do to help those struggling with homosexuality? We can open our homes. One of the largest factors in my being able to leave homosexuality behind was living with a Christian family for a year. It gave me a chance to heal and it was like a second childhood for me. Many of the painful wounds I received in childhood were paved over by the love of my host family. I learned how a husband and father is supposed to act in love toward his wife and children and how they are supposed to return that love, things I had never seen demonstrated. I learned about all the different relationships within a family, relationships that many take for granted, but relationships I never had. In many ways and on many levels, my time spent with that family healed me.

The family is a precious gift, a special institution. A healthy family with a loving father and mother can give so much to children, or even to an outsider like me who only stays for a short time. Though I only spent a year with them, my time with my host family gave me a foundation and a support from which I began to rebuild my life. Ecclesiastes 4:12 says, "Though one may be overpowered, two can defend themselves. A cord of three strands is not quickly broken." And how much stronger is the shelter of a family?

The church has long been accused of being homophobic because we have condemned homosexuality as a sin. While we are only trying to follow Scripture in most cases, we forget that words require actions as well. How can we blatantly accuse others of sin without offering a way out, an alternative? I believe that nothing will demonstrate the love of Christ more than if we open our homes to those in the homosexual lifestyle who sincerely want to leave it behind.

In practical terms, this type of ministry will not work if the person involved in homosexuality does not truly want to leave. Neither will it work if the host family is dysfunctional or not following the Word of God. There are multiple other factors to consider as well. Not every family is called to host someone in their home, whether they are trying to leave homosexuality or not. But surely there are Christian families that love Christ and are willing to open their lives, their marriages, and their families to minister to the hurting. Church, put out the call from the pulpits for families to step forward.

Obviously, the path toward healing and restoration may be a little different for each person. Not every homosexual individual wanting to leave the lifestyle should or wants to stay with a family for any length of time. There are many types of ministries that help gays and lesbians that don't involve staying with a family and they need an influx of volunteers, support, and prayer as well. (For more information on some of those ministries, please refer to the listing in the back of this book.)

Finally, as Christians, we need to remember to pray for those around us. Jesus said in Matthew 7:7–8, "Ask and it will be given to you; seek and you will find; knock and the door will be opened to you. For everyone who asks receives; he who seeks finds; and to him who knocks, the door will be opened." The apostle James also said this in James 5:13–20:

> Is any one of you in trouble? He should pray. Is anyone happy? Let him sing songs of praise. Is any one of you sick? He should call the elders of the church to pray over him and anoint him with oil in the name of the Lord. And the prayer offered in faith will make the sick person well; the Lord will raise him up. If he has sinned, he will be forgiven. Therefore confess your sins to each other and pray for each other so that you may be healed. The prayer of a righteous man is powerful and effective.
>
> Elijah was a man just like us. He prayed earnestly that it would not rain, and it did not rain on the land for three and a half years. Again he prayed, and the heavens gave rain, and the earth produced its crops. My brothers, if one of you should wander from the truth and someone should bring him back, remember this: Whoever turns

a sinner from the error of his ways will save him from death and cover over a multitude of sins.

Pray that God will raise up godly men and women in our churches, our homes, our workplaces, our schools, and in every place in our society. Pray for the love of God to be shown daily through their lives. Pray that many would turn from their sins and come to the saving knowledge of Jesus Christ through the power of their testimony.

Why does the issue of homosexuality matter? Why is it my business what someone else does in the privacy of their home?

The issue of homosexuality matters first and foremost because God said it mattered in His Word. It is not an issue that allows us to sit on the sidelines and think about whether or not it is a moral gray area. It is laid out in Scripture in black-and-white terms as a sin, and if it exists as a part of a believer's life, both that believer and his or her church need to address that homosexual temptation and activity.

God established heterosexual marriage at Creation as the foundation for all future societies. Our governments, our laws, our cultures, our churches, our schools, and our families are all based, in theory and in practice, on a heterosexual marital union. As much as any gay rights activist may want to change this fact for the future, the truth is that society in general, and our society in particular, has always had marriage between one man and one woman as a foundation throughout history.

Life itself is the product of the union of one man and one woman. Not a single one of us exists today because two women or two men came together. Children are only possible through heterosexual intercourse. A heterosexual, monogamous, and lifelong commitment through marriage is also the healthiest environment in which to raise children.

Even with high divorce rates, the majority of children are raised with a mother and a father. They learn how to interact with the world around them through the way they see their parents act. Each and every relationship children will eventually have throughout the entire course of their lives will in some way relate back to what they learned from their parents. Overwhelmingly, heterosexual marriage has been the filter through which children learn, view their world, and interact with society since the beginning of time.

The stability of our families is the stability of our society. We have seen in recent years the effects of premarital sex, single parent homes, adultery, and divorce on children. I grew up in a broken home; I know what it is like to wonder why your family can't be normal, what it is like to struggle financially, and what it is like growing up not being able to trust anyone but yourself. My childhood most certainly affected my adulthood and many of the problems I had could be traced back in some way to the instability of my family life. Now, my unstable childhood by no means excuses me from taking responsibility for my actions, but it certainly didn't prepare me to conduct my friendships and relationships in a healthy manner, or to make good decisions for my well being.

How does all of this relate to homosexuality? Homosexuality undermines what we have come to call traditional marriage. How? Homosexuality is no longer just about what two people do in the privacy of their own home because Gay/Lesbian/Bisexual/Transgender (GLBT) activists have turned it into a campaign to normalize and legalize gay marriage. If gay marriage becomes legalized, what has been the foundation in society for thousands of years, marriage between one man and one woman, will crumble at an even more alarming rate.

Let me explain. The idea of marriage has already been crumbling at an alarming rate since the free love of the sixties. Paternal and spousal responsibilities have been minimized while sexual freedom and promiscuity have been glorified. No-fault divorce laws have made it easier to obtain a divorce and have turned lifelong commitment into an optional consideration. The mindset has become that if the marriage doesn't work out, couples shouldn't try to fix it, they shouldn't try to work something out; instead, they should just start over. We have become accustomed to convenience and choice in every area of our lives and we have wrongly and tragically assumed that sexual freedom without constraint will also make our lives better.

The legalization of homosexual marriage will only add to the disintegration of traditional marriage. Traditional marriage and family, which have been the glue of society for so long, will become only one of many choices. We can see it start to come unglued already, but homosexual marriage will further push the family, and by consequence, society, into the unknown.

The vast majority of today's families are heterosexual, whether they are single-parent or not. What would happen to our society if, over a period of time, half of all families were made up of two individuals of the same sex? How would simple and daily relationships between men and women in the workplace, school, church, and society be affected? We simply don't know. Are we really willing to take such a chance just for the sake of social experimentation, all in pursuit of the illusion of "progress"?

There have been countless studies documenting the effect of divorce on children. It can devastate them, inflicting wounds that get buried deep and get carried throughout life. The lack of a father or mother figure can seriously impact every future relationship that child might have. Will having two mothers or two fathers be able to replace what was lost? No. There are certain things every child learns from a father that they cannot learn from a mother, and vice versa.

In addition, homosexual couples cannot reproduce. For most gay and lesbian couples who have children, one of the partners has brought the children over from a previous heterosexual relationship or marriage; infant adoption is far from the norm. The children in such cases are then forced to replace their father with another mother, or their mother with another father. What kind of messages about relationships and sexuality are being sent by the sudden change? And how will such a drastic change affect that child's future?

I can assure you from my own experience, as well as that of my partners, that homosexuality is far from monogamous. Homosexuality is too much of a search for self-identity and self-fulfillment for it to be satisfied by one person, especially a person of the same sex and emotional makeup. That desire will never be fulfilled, that search will never end, because same-sex relationships will not provide the answer for questions about identity and worth. Unfortunately, it is difficult to come to such a conclusion while in the midst of a homosexual lifestyle. For years, my answer when things didn't work out was simply to find another partner. I know my story is not unique in that regard for those involved in homosexuality. Because of that, children with homosexual parents are more likely to be exposed to a steady stream of new parental figures in their lives, which will be both confusing and damaging in their development.

We cannot let the family unit break down any further than it has already. I believe we must not only strongly oppose the legalization of homosexual marriage, but also rebuild the areas of marriage and family that have broken down. Responsibility in fatherhood needs to be taught and practiced more often so the number of fatherless homes is drastically reduced. We also need to reemphasize that sex should wait until marriage, marriage should last for life, and adultery is never acceptable. God gave us these rules as protection so that by following them, we will live happier and healthier lives.

In what other ways does homosexuality affect us? Once again, I would like to point out that homosexuality is no longer just about what two people do in the privacy of their own home, but it has been transformed into a legal, political, educational, and cultural campaign for the acceptance and legalization of same-sex marriage.

You can see the effects of the same sex marriage campaign in nearly every corner of our society. Many court cases are now making their way through our judicial systems and in some states, some judges are ruling in favor of domestic partnerships, same-sex benefits, and same-sex marriage licenses. In response, as of the writing of this book, nineteen states have amended their state constitutions to define marriage as being only between one man and one woman, and twenty-one states have passed into legislation state Defense of Marriage Acts (DOMA), which also define marriage as being between one man and one woman. On the other end of the spectrum, in 2004, Massachusetts began allowing same-sex couples to obtain marriage licenses. Quite obviously, at least in the political and legal arenas, homosexuality has become a "hot-button issue" and is affecting a large number of people throughout the United States. I believe it will continue to affect our nation for the next several election cycles until it is decided one way or another.

In order to gain supporters for their agenda of legalizing same-sex marriage in political and judicial forums, homosexual activists are working in other areas by trying to normalize the gay lifestyle into mainstream culture. The media is saturated with gay characters, themes, and promotions. There is a "token" gay character in nearly every TV show, usually portrayed as humorous, artsy, well dressed, and intelligent. Many films also feature homosexual characters, and in recent wide-release films such as *Alexander* and *Brokeback Mountain,* an attempt to show the normality of homosexuality has been much of the driving force of the plot. The gay lifestyle is glorified as being glamorous and is rarely shown as it really is—a lonely and painful search for love and identity.

Our children are also being brought into the debate. Health and sex education classes are now teaching the homosexual lifestyle as a viable alternative to marriage and family and are encouraging students to experiment sexually. Some guidance counselors are suggesting to confused adolescent students that their sexual uncertainties could mean they are gay. Even younger children are being exposed to homosexuality with books like *Heather Has Two Mommies* being used to teach children to read.

Homosexual culture and values have been making their way into our schools for a long time, and for good reason. Gay and lesbian activists know that even if they lose the culture war now, they will win it in twenty years by influencing the education of the next generation. If they can convince an entire generation that homosexuality is both normal and healthy, they will have more than enough political capital to change our society forever.

Churches are also feeling very real pressure to change their doctrines concerning homosexuality because of the lobbying of the gay activists. Some members of the church have listened to what our culture says about homosexuality and have decided that it is acceptable, but others have held fast to the Word of God and have made no excuse for sin. The debate over homosexuality has torn churches and even whole denominations apart. Unless we turn immediately back to God and His Word, we will continue to see the effects of this growing split for years to come. Some churches will continue to be accepting of sin and become little more than social clubs to ease the conscience, while the remaining churches will be ridiculed for their unwillingness to stray from Scripture no matter what the cost. In that day, righteousness and purity will become laughed at, old-fashioned, and obsolete, and many hearts will be hardened in their sin against God. Let me warn you, that day is not far off.

Homosexuality affects us already in so many ways, and it will continue to affect both our children and us in the future. If certain laws come into effect, including the legalization of same-sex marriage and certain hate crime bills, the future of our society could become very different. Churches could be sued or lose their tax-exempt status for refusing to perform same-sex marriage ceremonies or for refusing to hire gay parishioners. Companies will be forced to provide same-sex benefits. Our entire system of laws will have to be rewritten to accommodate homosexual unions. (And in the rewriting of those laws, who knows what else will change?) Parents will be forced to send their children to schools where homosexuality is taught and encouraged. It may even become illegal or considered a hate crime to publicly disagree with homosexuality or to quote a Bible verse that does. The importance and the practice of traditional marriage and family will deteriorate further and that disintegration will cause further problems in our society.

The issue of homosexuality is clearly an important and pressing subject that needs to be addressed. It isn't just about what two people do in the privacy of their own home, but it is also about the future of our society, the importance of marriage, the education of our children, and what is right and wrong in the eyes of God. The stakes are high and the final outcome of this debate will affect every person, whether they ignore the issue or not. For that reason, homosexuality matters and it becomes our business to become informed and to act out on our beliefs.

I encourage you to think critically and carefully about the issue of homosexuality, its potential impact, and the importance of resolving the debate quickly. Pray for our nation and its leaders that God will give them wisdom and courage to do what is right. And if you can, in your own way, let your voice be heard in your church, school, and community. It does matter and it will make a difference.

What about heterosexual promiscuity and sexual practices? Isn't there a double standard?

There is a double standard, but there shouldn't be. God calls each and every one of us to righteousness and purity. Part of that purity includes sexual purity. Homosexuality isn't the only sexual sin, but the church sometimes acts like it is because it doesn't want to address the issues of premarital sex, adultery, pornography, and lust, all of which are serious problems in churches.

Again and again I say this: pastors, preach righteousness from your pulpits. It is not acceptable for the body of Christ to stray into these sexual sins. Each of these sins have consequences and we are seeing their effects in the number of both fatherless homes and divorces. It needs to stop.

Jesus said this in Matthew 5:27–29:

> "You have heard that it was said, 'Do not commit adultery.' But I tell you that anyone who looks at a woman lustfully has already committed adultery with her in his heart. If your right eye causes you to sin, gouge it out and throw it away. It is better for you to lose one part of your body than for your whole body to be thrown into hell."

In other words, we need to do whatever it takes to make sure we do not fall into sin. Whatever is causing you temptation, cut it out of your life. Jesus also makes the very real point that our heart will determine the course of our actions. Will it not be much easier to commit adultery if we have dreamed about it and desired it already in our hearts? That dream and desire is called lust, which is also a sin.

We are hypocritical to accuse the homosexual of sin when we ourselves are also engaged in consistent sin, be it sexual or not. We must repent in our own lives and retake the moral ground we once held, not for the sake of accusing homosexuals of sin, but because we too must some day stand before God and account for everything we have done. So then, let us once again sound the call for righteousness and purity in our own lives.

Is homosexuality a civil rights issue?

Homosexuality is *not* a civil rights issue—*absolutely not.*

I was born black. I became a lesbian. They are *not* the same.

I did not choose the color of my skin. I did choose to enter a lesbian relationship and to live a homosexual lifestyle for fourteen years. I also chose to leave that lifestyle, but I cannot choose to stop being black. There is a difference. The color of my skin is an immutable quality of my being while my lesbianism was a deliberate series of actions resulting in a lifestyle choice.

It is a mockery to everything blacks suffered and the rights we won to claim that homosexuality is a civil rights issue. There is simply no comparison. Gays and lesbians have never been forced to ride at the back of the bus or to eat at separate restaurants. They didn't attend separate schools. They have never been made slaves or been considered by law as less than human. The African-American church needs to stand up for itself on this issue because, even though I am a former lesbian, as an African-American I am insulted that the homosexual community would even attempt to compare gay rights to civil rights.

Homosexuals have every single right that heterosexuals have—each right is exactly the same. They have the right to vote and be counted, not as three-fifths of a person, but as a whole person. They have the right to own property and they also have the right not to be property. They have the right to learn to read and to obtain an education. They have the right to eat at any restaurant, shop at any store, and enter any public place they wish. They have the right to cross state lines without fear of being hunted, beaten, and imprisoned. They have the right to let their voices be heard without being lynched. These are all rights blacks had to fight for through hundreds of years of struggle, but homosexuals do not deal with *any* of these civil rights issues.

Again, there is absolutely no comparison. Gay rights activists will cite the tragic and gruesome death of Matthew Shepherd, which was wrong in every sense of the word. However, Shepherd's death was an isolated incident and was not because he was gay; his murderers admitted it was a robbery.

Even now, so-called homophobia pales in comparison to racism. Homosexuals are not routinely pulled over by police at a higher rate than heterosexuals. Neighbors will not complain about a gay couple living next-door decreasing the value of the houses in their neighborhood. Very few people will become frightened if approached by a homosexual on the street. Employment and educational opportunities, as well as standards of living, are much higher for homosexuals than they are for blacks.

Blacks cannot hide their blackness; it is apparent to everyone who sees them. However, not everyone who looks at a homosexual will be able to determine their sexual orientation. The difference between black skin and homosexuality is that black skin is a physical characteristic while homosexuality is a behavior.

Put simply, there is no civil rights struggle for homosexuals. While there is some validity to claims of discrimination based on sexual orientation, it has been blown far out of proportion. I have suffered far more discrimination for being a black woman than I ever did for being a butch lesbian. Many claims of homophobia are intended to create a victim mentality within the homosexual community and a belief that homosexuals are oppressed in society at large. This tactic has played well in media circles and in political arenas and has gained many supporters for the normalization of the homosexual lifestyle and the campaign for same-sex marriage. However, the desire for the legitimization of a lifestyle does not equal a struggle for existence and equal rights. Homosexual rights are not, nor should they be considered as, a civil rights struggle.

In October 2005, I lobbied in Washington DC against a "Hate Crimes Bill" that was trying to make its way through the Senate and House. If it had been signed into law, the bill, S. 1145, would have expanded the legal definition of a minority group to include groups that share a similar behavior, with sexual orientation being an example of shared behavior. By painting such a broad definition of a minority group, the legislation would have made the term meaningless. If a behavior such as sexual orientation makes a community a minority group, then any group that exhibits similar behavior could qualify. It is conceivable that any person could make a claim to belonging to a minority group based on shared behavior with as little as one other individual. Crimes against a minority group count as a hate crime, the conviction of which carries an increased judicial sentence by law.

S. 1145 also claimed that in expanding the definition of a minority group, it would erase the memory of slavery. Such a claim is as ridiculous as it is foolish. The very idea that the memory of slavery would, could, or should be erased is a slap in the face of every black living in the United States. If we erased the memory of slavery, we would erase the proud history of the civil rights movement, we would erase the uniqueness of black culture, and we might doom ourselves to repeat the sins and tragedies of the past.

Hate crime bills that attempt to legally associate sexual orientation with race are but another attempt to promote the false idea that there are homosexual civil rights. S. 1145 failed, as have many other bills of the same type, but I don't doubt that similar bills will be tried in the future.

As a member of the black community, I believe it is time for us to stand up for ourselves and our heritage. Black churches seem to be ignoring homosexuality more than any other group of Christians, perhaps because we don't want to admit that it could happen in our families and in our churches. While it is important for us to minister and reach out to individuals struggling with homosexuality, we also need to stand against the progression of homosexuality in our society. That is a message the black church and community must verbalize. I want to encourage every black person reading this book to make it known to your government officials, to your churches, and to society that trying to make homosexuality seem normal is not and never will be the same thing as our long and hard struggle for civil rights.

The color of my skin is something I cannot alter, but God's gentle call and His love changed my life. His love was reflected through the obedience of a woman in a grocery store, a women's Bible study, and a family willing to take me into their home. I want to encourage churches, both black and white, to come together to send out a consistent message about homosexuality, one that speaks and acts in love while not compromising values or becoming accepting of sin. This we can do by making our own hearts and lives right with God and then by following the Holy Spirit's direction by ministering to those who struggle with homosexuality. I truly believe that what God has done in my life, He can do in the lives of all who call on His name.

What about same-sex marriage?

Same-sex marriage is a very hotly contested issue in our country and I want to take a little time to point out some things that should be considered during the course of the debate. As I mentioned in previous pages, same-sex marriage has the potential to radically change the basic foundation of our society, affecting relationships, education, government, churches, and society as a whole. These changes are unpredictable and risky because they fundamentally alter what has always been our definition of marriage and they escort us into an unknown and unproven area of social experimentation.

I talked briefly about what the definition of marriage could mean to the future of our society, but I would like to expand on that theme. The legalization of same-sex marriage would open the floodgates to even further changes of marriage. After all, if we redefine marriage once, why not do it again? If you change the definition of marriage from one man and one woman in a lifelong, monogamous relationship to two people in a lifelong, monogamous relationship, the rest of the definition is also subject to change.

Consider the logic behind the push for same-sex marriage. One of the major questions used in this argument is, If two people love each other, why can't they get married? While this argument might seem harmless, the same argument could easily and already is being adopted by other groups seeking to further expand the meaning of marriage.

If same-sex marriage is legalized, one of the next groups to seek societal approval will be pedophiles. The North American Man/Boy Love Association (NAMBLA) is one such group that wants to further redefine sexual norms and eventually marriage. NAMBLA promises to work closely with GLBT activists to draw attention to the issue of "ageism," which is discrimination based on age. Their website states that "membership is open to everyone sympathetic to personal freedom. Our goal is to end the oppression of men and boys who have freely chosen, mutually consensual relationships."[1]

There is nothing preventing NAMBLA or any other group promoting pedophilia from using the same arguments for their cause that the homosexual community is currently using. They fully intend to ride the coattails of homosexual activism. Already they are claiming that pedophilic relationships are mislabeled as taboo by society and that pedophiles are being oppressed. They use the argument, If two people love each other, why can't they be in a relationship? They are also trying to "promote awareness about ageism," which is NAMBLA's equivalent to homophobia.

Please understand that I am not saying that homosexuals are pedophiles, or that homosexuality causes pedophilia. My point is that pedophiles will use the same methods as the homosexual community to rationalize and normalize their behavior. I have little doubt that if our society continues its present course, pedophiles will begin to claim they were born that way, even if they have no scientific basis for their claim. There will be an increase in positive portrayals of pedophilic relationships in the media. There will also be a push in the courts and legislatures for the age of consent to be lowered or even eliminated completely. After all, what is age but a number? they will argue.

Another issue that will be raised and will demand attention will be group marriage, which includes polygamy (marriage between one man and more than one woman), polyandry (marriage between one woman and multiple men), and groups of multiple partners of both sexes. HBO has aired

---

1 http://www.nambla.org/

a show called *Big Love*, a show about the struggles and life of a polygamist family in Utah. Again, the strategy for the legalization of group marriage will be similar to the one for same sex marriage. It will be argued that limiting marriage as being only between two people is too narrow and restrictive. At which point the activists will argue, If a group of people is willing to commit to a lifelong and monogamous relationship, why shouldn't they be afforded the same rights as groups of two?

Incest will also see its own activists. If two people love each other, why does it matter if they are from the same family? It will be argued that advances in science have eliminated or greatly reduced the possibility of having children with serious birth defects. Again, the same methods will be used to normalize and integrate incest into our society as one of many options available in exploring sexual freedoms.

The list goes on. While it may seem ridiculous, bestiality, or sex with animals, will also try to make its way into the ever-expanding definition of marriage and relationships. Perhaps discrimination against those who wish to have sex with animals will be called specieism. If two beings love each other, do they not deserve the same rights given to everyone else?

Another possible redefinition of marriage could include the elimination of the term *lifelong*, which could have several different consequences. It is possible that marriage licenses could expire after a pre-arranged time limit, such as five or ten years. Although renewal would probably be an option, a marriage license with a time limit would have a similar effect as a divorce, especially if there are children. The time limit could also seriously destabilize the relationship.

Monogamy is another term that could be removed from the definition of marriage, as people will not want to limit their sexual freedoms with such an old-fashioned concept. Although it would seem there would be little point in being married if there is no monogamy, the redefinition of marriage could eventually be reduced to a legal recognition of a relationship. In all probability, if the definition of marriage were reduced to such a low point, it would become little more than a way to share benefits with someone who has a well-paying job.

While pedophilia, group marriage, incest, and bestiality are all currently illegal, considered taboo, and may seem incredibly far from being legalized or even normal, remember that fifty years ago homosexuality was also in a similar situation. However, the success of homosexual activism will pave the way for all of these other issues and will make it much easier for them to make their way into our society. The same blueprint will be used for each and every one:

- claim discrimination and oppression to form a civil rights campaign,

- draw attention and sympathy,

- desensitize the culture by continuous media exposure,

- normalize the behavior as a healthy and inborn quality,

- and finally, a campaign in the courts and legislatures.

If same-sex marriage is legalized, we will have little success arguing against the further redefinition of marriage. It is foolish to think the same arguments and strategies won't be used again and again to condone every type of sexual perversion and behavior. Some may be further away from being realized and accepted on a wide basis, but time and repeated exposure could change the minds of many people.

The legalization of same-sex marriage acts as a societal stamp of approval for immorality. In and of itself, same-sex marriage would have drastic and lasting effects on our society. When the rest of the sexual rights issues that will follow are also taken into consideration, it becomes imperative to stop the redefinition of marriage before it starts.

Should homosexual couples be allowed to adopt?

Adoption by homosexual couples is closely related to and is awaiting the legal resolution to the issue of same-sex marriage. Just as same-sex marriage is the goal of current homosexual activism, so the broad legalization of homosexual adoption will be the logical and natural outcome of same-sex marriage. If same-sex marriage becomes legal, adoption by those couples will increase as well. As of the writing of this book, there are currently nine states that allow adoption by homosexual couples, five states that either partially or completely ban it, and sixteen states that have pending legislation to ban it.

When I was living in the lesbian lifestyle, I had two partners who had children. I love children, but my lifestyle prevented me from having my own, and so I tried to make the most of the time I had with my partners' children. I loved them as my own children and my partners and I certainly had many conversations about adoption. Despite my lifestyle choice, I wanted so badly to have a normal family and adoption was the closest I would have been able to come to a traditional family.

I never did adopt my partners' children and, as I look back, I know it is better that I didn't. My relationships never lasted and, had I adopted, the children would have been subjected to a revolving door of new parental figures from their biological mothers and from me. As much as I wanted to adopt, I was never able to provide the type of stability their fathers could have provided, especially if the marriages had stayed intact.

I was tough, strong, and hard since childhood. However, those qualities weren't the product of my femininity; they were the result of all the pain and abuse I had suffered. I have since learned that true feminine strength and toughness are far different from the strength and toughness I had shown even only a decade ago. I did the best I could in helping raise those children, but it wasn't enough. In my own life, I never had a healthy example of a father figure and there was little chance of me being able to get it right without having seen what it was supposed to look like. I tried to imitate masculinity because of my own insecurity and desire to protect myself. It failed miserably in my life and it was that imitation I tried to display and teach to the children I had all but legally adopted.

The desire to have children is a natural instinct for nearly everyone, heterosexual and homosexual alike. However, my own childhood experiences have taught me that fathers are extremely important and my experiences in a lesbian parenting situation have taught me that I was no substitute for a father. Based on my own life, I would never be able to advocate for the cause of homosexual adoption, but there is far more to consider than just my testimony.

Unlike same-sex marriage, homosexual adoption most certainly affects more than just the two people involved.

Children are the future of our society and it is important for us to place those who have no families into the most stable environment we possibly can. By far, the healthiest and most stable environment will be for children to be with their biological parents. Absent that possibility, however, the next best option is still a heterosexual married couple.

Placing a child in a homosexual environment will severely hinder and confuse the development of that child's sexual identity. How will two lesbian women teach their daughter to date men? Or how will two gay men be able to guide their daughter through puberty and the onset of all the changes in her body? While the homosexual parents may be sympathetic and do their best, they will have no personal experience from which to draw to offer advice and empathy. Aside from the stability issues presented by the shaky nature of homosexual relationships, the ability of the homosexual parents to relate to their children is doubtful at best.

The truth is that the masculine and the feminine were created to complement each other in every way. The weaknesses of one are the strengths of the other. Men may be more logical and objective at times, but women are often able to relate and empathize easier. Many men may think they have an innate sense of direction, but women are more willing to ask for directions or look at a map. The male world is largely based on competition, but the female tends more toward cooperation. In just about every area of life, men and women approach problems and situations in different ways. By having examples of both masculine and feminine approaches to life, a child is better equipped to deal with whatever comes their way because they will have that many more tools available.

The gender roles in homosexual relationships often revert to mirror those of heterosexual relationships. One partner becomes more masculine, the other more feminine. This reversion occurs because it is natural for there to be one masculine and one feminine individual in each relationship. In the case of homosexual relationships however, the imitation is imperfect and the partners are trying to force themselves into unnatural emotional and gender roles.

A set of homosexual parents will never be able to provide the well-rounded and diverse view of problem-solving skills, interpersonal abilities, and wholesome sexual and self-identities to children that healthy heterosexual married couples offer. Each gender has something unique to offer to children, but two parents of the same gender will deprive the child of valuable life lessons because both parents will be speaking the same message. The child's picture is incomplete because the puzzle pieces simply do not fit together.

Conservatives have described homosexual adoption as the "second front" in the culture war, and I agree. As same-sex marriage gets closer to legalization, you will hear more and more about homosexual adoption. We need to ensure the safety of our children's futures and take a hard stand against adoption into "alternative families." I lived as a lesbian in several relationships that involved children, but even with my history and even though I loved those children, I believe the best possible environment for adopted children is for them to be part of a family that has as its foundation a lifelong, monogamous marriage relationship between one man and one woman.

What about the general acceptance of homosexuality in our culture?

I do *not* believe there is a general acceptance of homosexuality in our culture. However, I *do* believe the media and homosexual activists have worked very hard to make it *appear* as if there is a broad acceptance of homosexuality. I also believe that the desire to appear politically correct (and perhaps the fear of being labeled politically incorrect) has caused many people to remain silent about homosexuality even though they disagree with it in every way.

The media's positive portrayal of homosexuality does not in any way mean our culture is willing or ready to accept homosexuality on a broad basis. Consider *Brokeback Mountain,* a 2005 movie release that critics claimed was one of the greatest American love stories ever. Though it earned a respectable $178 million in box office sales worldwide,[2] this number falls far short of what such a critically acclaimed film should earn. Why wouldn't people want to see one of the greatest love stories ever? Because there is a disconnect between homosexuality and mainstream culture. The majority of Americans voted with their pocketbooks and elected not to see the movie.

Americans also voted in the polls and the results were the same. To date, twenty-seven states have amended their state constitutions with a Defense of Marriage Act (DOMA), which defines marriage as being between one man and one woman. In every state, the amendment has been voted on by the state's population, *not* the state's legislature. The amendment has passed in every single state it has been voted on (with the exception of Arizona), and in large percentages.

---

2 A further breakdown of box office numbers for Brokeback Mountain is available at http://boxofficemojo.com/movies/?id=brokebackmountain.htm

The amendment failed in Arizona by a small margin with 48 percent of the population favoring the position that marriage is a relationship specifically between one man and one woman. Mississippi had the highest percentage of 86 percent, and the average percentage of all twenty-eight states, including Arizona, in which an amendment was voted on was 68 percent in favor of a DOMA amendment to the state constitution. Every other state has some sort of DOMA legislation with the exception of Connecticut, Delaware, Massachusetts, New Mexico, New York, Rhode Island, Vermont, and Wyoming. Massachusetts is currently the only state that issues same sex marriage licenses, although litigation is pending.[3]

It is clear that when presented with a choice, the majority of people choose *not* to support homosexuality with either finances or political backing. Very few people are willing to change what has been a cornerstone in our society. They *have* repeatedly elected to support traditional marriage, a covenant that has worked well since the beginning of time.

The problem has been, however, that a very small minority has been extremely vocal and effective in spreading their message. Homosexual activists have been highly successful in promoting a 'tolerant' worldview. Unfortunately, if the minority's vision of tolerance is realized, it will infringe on the rights and lives of the majority, changing the social and cultural landscape of our nation forever.

Tolerance does not mean acceptance, nor does it mean cooperation. There are fundamental differences between the goals of homosexual activists and the beliefs and practices of the majority of society. Those differences include the definition

---

3 For current statistics and information regarding the status of DOMA laws, visit www.domawatch.org

of family, the future of our way of life, and the education of our children. While we can be tolerant and agree to disagree, that does not mean we have to agree to whatever demands the homosexual community happens to make.

I would like to challenge anyone who is involved in producing any type of media to help counteract the misleading outspokenness of the homosexual agenda by creating pro-family media. The family is in a state of crisis and is coming under fire from several different directions: abuse, divorce, extra-marital activity, the homosexual agenda, media, and teenage pregnancy. We desperately need examples in media of healthy families, who are not afraid to stay together and work things out, even when problems arise. We need to work together to keep whole an institution that has worked well for thousands of years. We need to spread the message that marriage is between one man and one woman and that marriage for life is for the best. We need to act quickly and vocally before we are no longer able to voice our concerns and act out on our beliefs.

What about homosexuality in schools?

The education of our children is perhaps the most important area that will affect the future of the family in the coming years. A child's education comes from several areas, starting with parents, but also extending to family, friends, media, and for a large part of life, school. I have spent time addressing many of those areas, but I would like to talk about school specifically and the messages today's children are receiving about their sexuality.

Nearly every public school has some sort of club for students with gender confusion issues, including but not limited to GLBT groups, P-FLAG (Parents, Families, and Friends of Lesbians And Gays), and the Gay-Straight

Alliance. Many school counselors, if a student comes to them with questions about their sexual identity, will refer them to one of these groups. The problem is that many students naturally have questions about their sexual identity because they are going through adolescence.

Questioning your sexual identity doesn't mean you are gay. Adolescence is a period filled with a great deal of uncertainty and it is a time when both peer and adult influences matter very much. I know that if I had joined a GLBT group while in high school, I very probably would have entered the homosexual lifestyle at an earlier age. I wonder how many students are making the same choice I would have because those groups are now available on a wider basis. I also wonder how many students wouldn't have chosen the homosexual lifestyle but for the influence of their school's GLBT club. The clubs teach and reinforce homosexual behavior to many who would perhaps have otherwise been able to reconcile their gender identity issues.

There is also dangerous curriculum in many health/sex-ed classes that encourage children to be sexually active at very young ages. Middle-school children are often handed contraceptives so they become familiar with their feel and use. While they are not always directly told to experiment sexually, that message is still passed along by the distribution of condoms and the lack of education about the importance of sexual abstinence until marriage. The mantra of many of our sex-ed classes has been, "If it feels good, do it, just be sure to use protection." That message is growing to include homosexual and bisexual experimentation.

The curriculum doesn't stop in the health class. In some classrooms, children are being taught to read with the help of books like *Heather Has Two Mommies* and *Daddy's*

Roommate. They are exposed to an even greater amount of literature sympathetic to homosexuality as they grow older. If homosexual activists had their way, gay literature and texts would come flooding into the school systems in all subject areas.

Colleges are far more open and insistent about the homosexual lifestyle than secondary schools. Openly gay teachers and faculty are quite common, as are those who approve of the gay agenda, and their beliefs are also taught in the classrooms. It is considered old-fashioned and narrow-minded to support traditional family values and ethics, and in some cases, students who do so are publicly reprimanded, ridiculed, or demeaned in their classes. Many of the women's studies classes are taught by lesbian professors and the girls who enroll in those classes come away with a distorted view of men, if not a willingness to explore their sexuality with other females because of their newfound fear and distrust of the opposite sex.

There is also an abundance of GLBT groups in colleges, and they are far more active and vocal than those in the secondary schools. The University of Minnesota, for example, routinely hosts gay and lesbian speakers and events. On National Coming Out Day, a door frame is set outside the student union and Goldie the Gopher, the school mascot, comes out of the closet by walking through the door, along with any other students who wish to announce their homosexuality. Every semester, the University of Minnesota also holds a separate graduation ceremony called "Lavender Graduation" for gay, lesbian, bisexual, and transgender seniors expected to graduate. Similar events and practices are echoed on college campuses throughout the country.

What are the effects of such an education on our children? They are being encouraged to explore their sexuality in unhealthy ways. The teaching in their homes and churches is being undermined and replaced by homosexual propaganda that some schools are teaching. Although homosexual activists will vehemently deny it, recruiting into the homosexual lifestyle or into supporting their goals is going on.

The behavior of our children is changing as well. Boys, who are more easily aroused by what they see, are becoming more and more fascinated with lesbianism. I have heard stories about high school and college parties and dances where girls (who are often drunk, though sometimes not) are egged on or paid by boys to make out or go even further with other girls. These girls aren't really lesbian or bisexual, but they are pretending to be so in order to gain the approval of the boys; it's become cool. Another fad making its way into colleges is the establishment of gay or lesbian dormitories.

Why does all this matter? Our children are our future and the future of our society. What we teach them will have an impact hundreds of years from now. No matter how many battles are won in legislatures, courts, and the media, the education of our children is the most important battleground. Five or ten years from now, it may be too late. We may win the culture war now only to lose it in the next generation.

A culture war? Is it really that bad?

When people talk about a culture war, they are talking about a war that has been going on for several decades. I want to emphasize here that the culture war is a war of *ideas*; it is not, nor should it ever be, a war against individuals. And yes, it is very serious and important, no matter which side you happen to be on, because the winner will determine the future course of our nation and society. So what ideas are competing against each other? To explain everything would require several books, but I will briefly explain as best I can.

Our nation was founded on certain moral principles and guidelines. While not forcing anyone to conform to a certain religion, the majority has practiced Judeo-Christian values and has held the Bible as the moral measuring stick for our society. God, church, marriage, family, hard work, education, and freedom, all of which are based on living according to biblical principles, have worked together to make the United States one of the richest, most powerful, and most blessed nations in the history of the world.

In recent years, however, some have decided they can improve our way of life by introducing new social norms. Unfortunately, "improvement" often means completely throwing away the traditional in favor of something new and untested, usually for the sake of convenience. As a consequence, many of the Biblical principles that have been a successful part of our society for so long have come under sharp criticism by those who wish to adopt a new way of life.

Homosexuality, same-sex marriage, and homosexual adoption are but a few of the many ideas that are seeking to replace our traditional and biblical ideas of family, church, and society. Other hotly contested issues are abortion, divorce, euthanasia, evolution, moral relativism, reproductive rights, and sexual freedom. Issues we will see more of in the future include cloning, incest, genetic experimentation and manipulation, group marriage, pedophilia, and stem-cell research. All of these issues are battlegrounds in the culture war, the war of ideas.

I believe the next ten to twenty years will have an incredible impact on the fate of our nation. We will be changing the shape and future of our society as each one of these battles is played out and either won or lost. There are certainly intelligent and good people on both sides of every issue, but again, I would like to point out the principles that have guided our nation to where it is today: we have honored God and obeyed His Word.

After such a history of blessing and success, let us not abandon our foundation for the untried and untrue; let us turn our hearts once more to God and to the principles found in Scripture. The consequences of not doing so will be disastrous because we will no longer enjoy God's hand of protection on our nation. If we do turn back, however, He will continue to bless us in every area of our lives.

What are the effects of a homosexual lifestyle?

For those reading this book who may be considering the homosexual lifestyle, let me tell you the truth: it isn't fun. It isn't glamorous. It isn't trendy. It doesn't fill the emptiness inside. It doesn't help you find your identity. It doesn't give you peace—and it never, ever will.

I lived as a lesbian for fourteen years, and now, by the grace of God, I have left that life behind forever. It wasn't enough for me. I had been so hurt and damaged as a little girl that I had grown to distrust men in general and black men in particular. I tried to fix my hurt by becoming someone I was never meant to be and it just didn't work. Lesbianism made me miserable. It was only by submitting myself to the almighty Creator of heaven and earth and allowing Him to reshape my life that I have begun to find healing and peace.

You see, every day I lived as a lesbian, I knew I was living a lie. I knew God had created man for woman and woman for man. I knew homosexuality was a sin. I knew God had a plan for my life. I knew all those things, but I ignored them as long as I could. I thought I could do better. I thought I could find my own solution to the hurt and pain and I went through drugs, smoking, bulimia, and lesbianism trying to find that solution.

When you are hurting so badly inside that you are willing to do anything, including going against what most of society considers normal by trying homosexuality, why not try God first? I buried my hurt, but that hurt became a monster inside of me, a gaping hole that devoured my happiness and peace, and it was never satisfied. It drove me to such depths and to such extremes that I am grateful even to be alive. I failed again and again in everything through which I tried to find a moment of happiness.

What are the effects of living a homosexual lifestyle? The list is long: Hurt. Despair. Frustration. Loneliness. Depression. Fear. Doubt. Desperation. Restlessness. Shame. I used to be afraid to fall asleep in case I died before I had turned back to God. I lived every day as someone I was not meant to be and my misery and attitude toward those around me and toward myself reflected that lie.

Hollywood would have you believe gays and lesbians are happy, humorous, and well-adjusted people, but very rarely do they show the other side—the ugly side. They don't show the hurt and pain beneath the armor. They don't show the tears behind the mask. They don't show the desperate ache to be loved beneath all the jokes, clever comebacks, and playful remarks.

When you give into homosexuality, you feel somehow twisted up inside, like something isn't right. You think you are doing the best thing for yourself because that is what society says, that you were born that way and that you just need to accept yourself, but it just doesn't feel right. You might try gay bars, you might meet a few people, you might begin several different relationships, you might smile on the outside, but on the inside? On the inside there is still a war going on.

You lay awake at night and wonder if you will ever have a family. You try to imagine a different world in which homosexuality is perfectly normal. Then you try to imagine a different life in which you had chosen to get married and have children. You wonder if you have chosen the right way by choosing homosexuality, but then you can't think of any way to leave it behind. There has to be some way to make it work, you tell yourself over and over again. Sometimes you remember being raped when you were a child and all the other abuses you suffered; you grow angry and scared at the same time, and then you try to forget they ever happened. At times you hate God and wonder why He created you to begin with, and then later you wish there was some way He could rescue you from the living hell that torments you.

My friends, learn from my life, my suffering, and my mistakes. Homosexuality will never feel comfortable; it will never be fun; it will never be the final destination in your search for love and acceptance. Even the sex doesn't feel natural or right. The pieces just don't fit together the way they do naturally for heterosexual sex. Even those who elect to get a sex-change operation must take hormones for the rest of their lives to change them into something they were not naturally.

I knew I was living a dirty and shameful life and there were better things out there, but I thought I was doing the best I could with what I had been given. I thought I was getting what I deserved. And maybe I was. God intervened with His mercy and grace. Grace is getting what you don't deserve, and God gave me both. God's love changed my life. He has changed my shame into His glory. He turned my weeping to laughter and my despair to peace.

To everyone considering or already living in the homosexual lifestyle, I lived your hurt, pain, despair, and loneliness; there is another way. God will not reject you if you turn to Him. You may have been hurt by those in the church or by those who claim to be Christians, but realize that God Himself still loves you. He wants to heal your hurt, mend your heart, and restore your joy. He is calling to you, and His call is one of love, but it is up to each one of us to answer that call.

Deuteronomy 30:19 says, "This day I call heaven and earth as witnesses against you that I have set before you life and death, blessings and curses. Now choose life, so that you and your children may live."

What about HIV and AIDS?

There are very few people in the homosexual community who do not know someone who has HIV or AIDS. There are also very few who do not know someone who has died from AIDS. I am no exception. My brother died from AIDS.

Though I have already told this story, I will tell it again because it bears repeating. My brother Robert turned to homosexuality while I was still in high school. We accepted our brother for who he was, but he grew apart from us as he went deeper into the homosexual lifestyle. When I moved away to college, I rarely saw or heard from him.

Years later, the family found out that Robert had been arrested and was going to prison for selling cocaine. Robert told me secretly that he had also contracted HIV. While he was in prison, Robert's HIV turned into full-blown AIDS, and Robert knew a clock had begun ticking down to his death. He made his own funeral arrangements and paid for his burial plot because he knew he was dying and he didn't want the family to know or to see him while his health rapidly deteriorated.

Robert was in the hospital because he needed a blood transfusion, but no transfusion in the world would have been able to help him. He was hooked up to an IV and another machine for his transfusion. His sheets were soaked in blood.

I still cry today, even years later, when I think of Robert's story, the way he lived and the way he died. I believe he turned to God before he died because he called my Aunt Mable just three days before his death and said that he had made things right with God. Even though he is now with Jesus, the message of Robert's life is one to pay attention to because it carries a warning.

Is AIDS God's judgment on the homosexual community as some claim? I don't know. That will have to be decided between God and them. What I do know is that HIV and the AIDS infection are very common in the homosexual community, so much so that gay men have a life expectancy significantly lower than heterosexual men. Insurance companies label homosexuality a high-risk lifestyle.

While homosexual organizations have raised millions of dollars for AIDS research (which I think is wonderful), there is also a section of the gay community that has gone in the opposite direction. There is actually an underground movement of gay men who seek to infect themselves with HIV or, as they call it, "the bug." Many of the gay men seeking the virus eroticize it, thinking that the moment of viral transmission is the ultimate moment of ecstasy. Others are merely resigned to their fate and want to control when they contract the virus. These men use the Internet and online discussion groups to contact other gay men who have tested HIV-positive. Within the homosexual community, those who want HIV are called "bug chasers," while those who are already infected are called "gift givers."[4]

HIV and AIDS are far from being erotic, and no disease should be considered a status symbol, especially when it leaves its victims sweating blood on a hospital bed as their lives quickly slip away. There is no cure for HIV or AIDS and therapy can only temporarily hold back the full-blown virus. Although it can be transferred through blood transfusions or sharing needles while taking illegal drugs, the most common form of HIV transmission is risky sexual behavior, which is rampant in the homosexual community. Contraceptives can only minimize the contraction risk; they do *not* eliminate it. Abstinence until marriage with an uninfected spouse is the only way to avoid contracting the virus sexually, a plan that God laid out in the Bible for our protection.

Can you really leave homosexuality?

Yes, a thousand times yes, it is possible to leave homosexuality! I tell everyone I can about the change God's love brought about in my life. I believe my testimony will give hope to many who are considering or struggling with homosexuality. There is another way out; you don't have to live in bondage any longer.

Jesus said this in John 8:34–36:

> I tell you the truth, everyone who sins is a slave to sin.
> Now a slave has no permanent place in the family, but

---

4 For more information on "bug chasing," contact the Center for Disease Control and Prevention or browse their website, www.cdc.gov. *Rolling Stone Magazine* also published a relevant article on Jan. 23, 2003 by Gregory A. Freeman entitled, "Bug Chasers: The Men Who Long to be HIV+".

a son belongs to it forever. So if the Son sets you free, you will be free indeed.

God is calling us into His family and He wants to set us free. Everyone who calls on the name of the Lord will be set free. Matthew 7:7–11 says:

> Ask and it will be given to you; seek and you will find; knock and the door will be opened to you. For everyone who asks receives; he who seeks finds; and to him who knocks, the door will be opened. Which of you, if his son asks for bread, will five him a stone? Or if he asks for a fish, will give him a snake? If you, then, though you are evil, know how to give good gifts to your children, how much more will your Father in heaven give good gifts to those who ask him!

I am not alone. There are many who share my story, who have come out of homosexuality by the grace of Jesus Christ. Let us be silent no more. It is time for our stories to be heard, for our testimonies to be witnessed, and for the world to know that our God is a God of miracles and love.

Is there freedom from temptation? What helped you most as you were called out of homosexuality?

Yes, there is freedom from temptation, and that goes for every area of your life, not just homosexuality. Does that mean temptation will never return, that you will never think about such things again? Of course not, but you can be free from giving into temptation. I know that in my own personal life, fleeing from temptation was a struggle and a journey, and it didn't happen overnight, but with God's power, I was able to learn how to resist.

First Corinthians 10:13 says:

No temptation has seized you except what is common to man. And God is faithful; He will not let you be tempted beyond what you can bear. But when you are tempted, He will also provide a way out so that you can stand up under it.

What is that way out? It may be a little different for each person, but I can tell you what helped me. When I first came back to God after living a homosexual lifestyle for fourteen years, God blessed me by placing me in a women's Bible study. Some of the women in that study became close friends and I was able to confide in them whenever I was tempted to go back to my lifestyle or even when I was tempted by having thoughts about other women. The process of being open and honest about my weaknesses helped me grow and it helped me conquer my temptations. James 5:13–16 says,

> Is any one of you in trouble? He should pray. Is anyone happy? Let him sing songs of praise. Is any one of you sick? He should call the elders of the church to pray over him and anoint him with oil in the name of the Lord. And the prayer offered in faith will make the sick person well; the Lord will raise him up. If he has sinned, he will be forgiven. Therefore confess your sins to each other and pray for each other so that you may be helped. The prayer of a righteous man is powerful and effective.

My advice would be this: Find someone godly you can trust, be it a close friend, a pastor, or a relative, and share with them about your temptations and your struggles. Ask them if they would be willing to keep you accountable. If you don't have anyone you can trust, ask God to send you someone.

Another thing that helped me was to stop living with my girlfriend. At the age of forty, I moved in with a Christian family (one of the women in my Bible study offered to let me stay), and it was as if I had a second childhood. I was subject to their rules, and I struggled against them a lot. I secretly saw my old girlfriend and called her on the phone because my sins were trying to reclaim me. Finally, my new "mother" told me that I couldn't have any more contact with my girlfriend or else I would be kicked out of the house. Reluctantly, I obeyed. Even though I didn't want to go back to my old lifestyle, the pull was very strong and I struggled for a while, but God gave me the strength to let go. James 1:13–15 says:

> When tempted, no one should say, "God is tempting me." For God cannot be tempted by evil, nor does He tempt anyone. But each one is tempted, when, by his own evil desire, he is dragged away and enticed. Then, after desire has conceived, it gives birth to sin, and sin, when it is full-grown, gives birth to death.

The lesson I learned was that I had to remove myself, as much as possible, from things that would tempt me. I could not leave the homosexual life and still live with the woman who had been my lesbian partner. If there is anything in your life that causes you to stumble, get rid of it. If you have triggers that cause you to think about men or women in ways that aren't right, whether parties, movies, pornography, or even certain friends, stay away from them. They will only call you back; they will only lead you back into temptation and eventually sin. Genesis 4:7 says, "If you do what is right, will you not be accepted? But if you do not do what is right, sin is crouching at your door; it desires to have you, but you must master it." If you have trouble leaving those things behind, talk to someone about it. Ask them to help you.

The final thing I will say is this: seek out God with all your heart. He can heal your broken heart; He can mend your wounds. He loves you. If you leave everything behind, all your temptations, all the things in your life that cause you to sin, but then don't replace them with God, they will only come back stronger. Jeremiah 29:11–14 says,

> "For I know the plans I have for you," declares the LORD, "plans to prosper you and not to harm you, plans to give you hope and a future. Then you will call upon me and come and pray to me, and I will listen to you. You will seek me and find me when you seek me with all your heart. I will be found by you," declares the LORD, "and will bring you back from captivity."

This is not to say you will never, ever be confronted again with temptation, but it means you are no longer in bondage to your sins the way you once were. When temptation comes again, you will know how to deal with it. Seek God's truth and it will set you free.

Have those who claim to have come out of homosexuality been brainwashed? Is the desire still there, but repressed because of what you've been taught by the church?

In no way have I been brainwashed, tricked, coerced, paid, or forced to leave homosexuality. I left homosexuality the same way I went in, by my own free will. I had to do it by my choice. No one could have made me leave it and nobody can make me go back. I now stand with the many others who share my testimony of leaving homosexuality.

Even though I made the choice to leave homosexuality, I had help. I honestly don't think I could have left my old lifestyle if I didn't have something better to run to. That something better for me was the love of Jesus Christ. Christ's love didn't brainwash me, but it did change me, and the change was for the better. He took the ashes of my old life and gave me new hope, new peace, and new love. Psalm 40:2–3 describes perfectly how I feel (NKJV):

> He also brought me up out of a horrible pit, out of the miry clay, and set my feet upon a rock, and established my steps. He has put a new song in my mouth—praise to our God; many will see it and fear, and will trust in the Lord.

I will freely admit that I lived as a lesbian for fourteen years, but that is no longer who I am. The transformation in my life does not mean I am denying some suppressed homosexual feelings or the core of my being. Since coming to Christ, I know who I am for the first time in my life and it feels wonderful. I am loved. I am free. I am called by my name and not by my shame. I no longer have to worry about being accepted because God has opened His arms wide and He has let me cry my pain away.

I don't have any repressed desires. I do sometimes think about what would have happened to my life if I had never left the homosexual lifestyle. Even though I think about my previous homosexuality at times, the desire to return is gone. It has been replaced with a desire to serve God, and I know that someday I will also have a husband.

I no longer live in fear of having to hide who I am. First John 4:18 says, "There is no fear in love. But perfect love drives out fear, because fear has to do with punishment. The one who fears is not made perfect in love." I am done with fear and I am done with shame. I now live for God. I make no apologies about my testimony and about what God has done in my life. In fact, I will continue to shout from the highest mountaintops and from the deepest valleys about the love and the grace of Jesus Christ and the profound and eternal impact He has made in my life for as long as I live.

In your story, you mention that you also struggled with drugs and bulimia. What advice do you have for those who struggle in those areas?

When you begin to struggle in one area of your life, sometimes it is very easy for that struggle to spill over into new battles and addictions. In my case, I struggled in a lot of different areas. The things I had problems with were very different in their outward appearance, but when I look back, I can see similarities between them.

My childhood had a lot to do with my decision to enter homosexuality, but it also had a profound impact on my drug use and battle with bulimia. My hurt and pain caused me to begin to search for happiness and love and I tried to do that in a variety of ways.

When I first began using drugs, I was just looking for a way to escape from the experiences of my life. Even if it was just for a moment, the high I felt was enough to make me think I was happy. However, there is a reason the feeling you get when you take drugs is called a "high" because there are also many, many lows. The lows I experienced made my life worse than it would have been without taking drugs, but because my high felt so good, I went back to the drugs again and again. It became a cycle and then an addiction.

My bulimia was also an attempt to escape, though in a slightly different way. I was never very confident about my appearance as a child. I looked and acted like a boy and everyone told me so. Several of my family members were overweight and I didn't want to become like them because I didn't want to give people another reason to ridicule me about the way I looked. As an adult, I wanted to be an instructor at a fitness club, but the manager told me I was too heavy and that I had to lose more weight before I could do so. Shortly after, a girl told me that I could control my weight by eating and purging. I tried to escape my fears and insecurities by seizing control of how I looked, but I did it in an unhealthy way and I fell into bulimia. Like my drug use, it became a cycle and I soon found I wasn't able to get out.

With any addiction, whether it is alcohol, bulimia, drugs, homosexuality, or pornography, my advice is to seek help. It is *so* hard to escape an addiction on your own and there are many people who are willing to help others overcome addictions. It really does help when you have people by your side, encouraging you, holding you accountable, and being your strength when you don't have any left.

Be prepared. It won't be easy to leave your addictions behind. It will take some time, a lot of prayer, and a lot of support. It takes courage to take that first step, but it is worth it and you will be grateful that you chose to take action. Freedom is worth the price of overcoming addiction.

Know that God loves you, no matter what you do, no matter what you look like. Your true self-worth is not and should not be measured by your appearance. You will never find yourself by taking any kind of narcotic. Drugs will never satisfy. They only distract your attention without addressing the problems. In fact, they create new problems.

As in everything, my advice is always to seek out God and run into His arms and turn your problems over to Him. He will surround you with His love and then, together, you will begin to face the areas in your life that need attention.

How can I help? What are some resources I can use to find out more about homosexuality?

Without the willing love and ministry of many, my life would be so much different. I know my story is not unique and there are others who have been impacted by individuals or ministries. To all who have already been so faithful: thank you. Keep the faith, keep fighting, keep loving, keep making a difference.

Now, to those who wish to help or find out more about homosexuality, there are some resources and websites in the back of this book that will direct you to further information about homosexuality or help you contact an existing organization if you wish to volunteer time, money, or prayer. I strongly encourage you to get involved in your church and if there is not an in-church ministry that reaches out to homosexuals, start one. If you need help talking with your church and setting up a ministry to homosexuals, feel free to contact my ministry (www.janetboynesministries.com) and we will try to help you begin.

If any of that sounds like too much to begin with, remember that we also covet your prayers. Pray that God will help us love the way He would have us love. Pray for those who are hurting. Pray that our ministries would make a difference in the lives of those God brings across our path and that we will always point everyone toward a deeper relationship with Jesus Christ. Pray for the state of our families and our marriages. Finally, pray that God will raise up strong, skilled, and godly men and women as leaders in government, church, media, education, and family. Thank you so much for your prayers.

What comes next for you? Will you ever get married?

God has truly been faithful. Within the last several years, I have been blessed with speaking opportunities at churches, conferences, on the radio, on television, in Washington DC, and even in Jerusalem. I hope to continue speaking and spreading the news that God's love has an amazing power to change lives and that homosexual orientation can be changed.

In 2006, Janet Boynes Ministries became an official non-profit organization and I can tell you that it is a lot of work. We also launched our Web site and hope to use it to coordinate our ministry. By God's grace, we hope to continue ministering to individuals who wish to leave the homosexual lifestyle and I pray we will also be able to teach churches about homosexuality and be able to help them set up their own ministries to the homosexual community.

As for what lies ahead, I am ever hopeful and eager to see what God has planned for me. I do desire to get married, but it isn't something I'm going to rush into, and so I'm waiting on God's perfect man, plan, and timing. But I know that my story isn't finished...